SIMPLY GOOD pasta

healthy fast food for busy people

Peter Sidwell

Also by Peter Sidwell:

Simply Good Taste
Simply Good Bread

Recipe notes:

All teaspoons and tablespoons are level.

Both metric and imperial measurements have been given in all recipes. Use one set of measurements only and not a mixture of both.

All cooking times are approximate and will vary in accordance with the type of cooker hob, conventional or fan oven used.

Please be advised this book includes recipes where nuts have been used.

Eggs should be medium unless otherwise stated.

First published in Great Britain in 2012 by Simon & Schuster UK Ltd
A CBS COMPANY

1 3 5 7 9 10 8 6 4 2

SIMON & SCHUSTER
ILLUSTRATED BOOKS
Simon & Schuster UK Ltd
222 Gray's Inn Road
London
WC1X 8HB

www.simonandschuster.co.uk

Simon & Schuster Australia, Sydney
Simon & Schuster India, New Delhi

Editorial director: Francine Lawrence
Project editor: Sharon Amos
Designer: Geoff Fennell
Photography: Richard Faulks
Cover photography: William Shaw
Production manager: Katherine Thornton
Commercial director: Ami Richards

A CIP catalogue record for this book is available from the British Library

ISBN 978-0-85720-270-3

Printed and bound in China
Colour reproduction by Dot Gradations Ltd, UK

SIMPLY GOOD
pasta

healthy fast food for busy people
Peter Sidwell

SIMON &
SCHUSTER
ILLUSTRATED

London · New York · Sydney · Toronto · New Delhi

A CBS COMPANY

Contents

Pasta - real fast food

Pasta is the one ingredient most people have in their cupboard. It's so familiar to us and it's a fantastic way of combining a few great seasonal flavours in one dish. The best thing about pasta is that it's a flavour carrier: you can literally just throw a few things into a pan, add some pasta and you've got supper. So this book is not about spending hours in the kitchen; it's about raiding the fridge and cupboards and creating a great-tasting dish that can be on the table quicker than you can heat up a frozen pizza. Lots of my recipes are real fast food. You put the pasta on to boil and make the sauce while the pasta is cooking. Simple!

As well as introducing you to simple, fast food, I've got another agenda. I want to combine our familiarity with pasta with good British seasonal ingredients. I want to bridge the gap between the two and inspire you to embrace the seasons and their produce. With these recipes my aim is to keep it simple and keep it British, while drawing on an international influence.

Too often, we end up cooking the same old dishes from a limited repertoire. People I talk to tell me they just stick to the same familiar recipes, winter, spring, summer and autumn. But if you take a little time to find out what ingredients are at their best right now, you can create a dish that is far more exciting and original.

My cooking is bold, gutsy and brave. And I want to give you the same confidence to put ingredients together to create a quick mid-week supper.

So come on, let's get cooking!

How to get the best from this book

If you've seen me on TV, you'll know I'm not big on using scales, but I have put weights and measures in my recipes just to get you started. To me cooking is a tactile thing: it's all about touch, feel and taste. Once you get the hang of it, you'll feel the same.

I always teach my trainee chefs to taste their cooking. So many people cook a dish and serve it without even tasting it. This point is crucial: it's the difference between an ok dish and a gob-smacking one that will leave a lasting memory – a dish that your family will be asking for again and again.

Key to my way of cooking is a well-stocked fridge. Mine is a source of inspiration for me – the secret is to keep it topped up. I fill my fridge up with yummy goodies from the local deli or supermarket – everything from crayfish tails to artichoke hearts – as well as simple but delicious homemade sauces and pesto.

Before you get started...
All my recipes serve four people.

Always check the instructions on the packet of pasta. I haven't given precise instructions every time as different manufacturers recommend slightly different cooking times. But, as a rule of thumb, spaghetti takes 9–10 minutes, pasta shapes anything from 9–12.

Most of the time I haven't specified a particular pasta shape – just use whatever you have in the cupboard. Where I've deliberately used spaghetti or penne, for example, try to stick to this if possible as it works really well with the sauce or ingredients.

First things first, get a big pan of boiling water on the heat and add a teaspoon of salt. The quicker the pan boils, the quicker you'll be sat down enjoying a cracking pasta dish.

You don't actually need to measure out a tablespoon of oil: just pour oil into the pan for as long as it takes to say '1 tablespoon'. If you add a little more it's not going to ruin the dish.

You're used to pre-heating the oven before you cook, right? Well, now apply the same principle and pre-heat your pan too – there's absolutely no point in starting to cook with a cold pan.

If I can find a way of using just one pan I will – you wouldn't believe I own a dishwasher!

In lots of my recipes I tell you to put the sauce ingredients into the pan you've cooked the pasta in.

Never use extra-virgin olive oil for cooking – it's a waste of flavour and money. Keep two sorts of oil in your store cupboard: a mild one for cooking and a fruity extra-virgin for adding to finished dishes or for making salad dressing.

Remember, seasonal food is the key to diversity. I like the fact that you can't buy pumpkins all year round.

In the standby favourites section you'll find my recipe for basic homemade pesto (plus lots of tasty variations). Pesto and pasta is a meal in itself. And I often tell you to add some pesto to my recipes. But if you haven't got round to making any, don't worry, just use readymade pesto from your local deli. The same goes for ricotta cheese – homemade is great but you can use shop bought instead.

Why waste heat? The residual heat in the pan warms the sauce without any risk of burning – and it saves on washing up.

Slow cookers are seen as a bit old hat, but the more I get into them, the better I think they are. It's a bit like having a mini Aga.

Whenever I tell you to whip the pasta pan back under the colander to catch the last few drops of cooking water, make sure you do it. It's a way of creating creaminess in a dish without actually adding any cream! It makes a real difference to the finish.

Always use fresh herbs. I never use dried. Well almost never – the only exceptions are tarragon, which isn't always easy to come by fresh, and very occasionally I use an Italian dried blend.

And add plenty of seasoning – I'd say 90 per cent of cooks don't use enough. Black pepper is a must.

Standby favourites

This chapter is all about stocking up your kitchen with loads of goodies that will give you the basics you need to create dishes from this book. People ask me all the time: how do I go home at the end of a hard day's teaching at my cookery school and start cooking all over again? Well, this chapter shows you just how easy it can be. The secret is to keep your options open and have a store cupboard and fridge full of ingredients just waiting for you to rustle something up.

Basic tomato sauce

This sauce is the secret to making life easier and taste better! If you can find time to make a batch in advance, it opens up a whole world of easy and exciting dishes. You can use it as the base for many different recipes – but it also tastes great on its own as a pasta sauce.

INGREDIENTS

4 x 400g (13oz) cans of chopped tomatoes

2 onions

6 garlic cloves

1 vegetable stock cube

handful of basil (if you haven't got fresh basil, add a few teaspoons of basil pesto – for homemade, see page 17)

salt and pepper

Here's how

Place the tomatoes in a large saucepan. Chop the onions and add to the pan, followed by the garlic. Don't worry about chopping the garlic cloves, just crush them with the back of your knife, peel the skin off and chuck the cloves into the pan. Crumble in the stock cube. Place the pan on a medium heat and let it simmer for 30 minutes until the onions are tender. (If you're in a hurry, chop the onions finely and they will cook quicker.)

When the onions are soft, turn off the heat. Use a stick blender to blend the sauce until it is nice and smooth. While you are blending, add the basil leaves and stalks.

Season with salt and pepper to your taste – I usually add a teaspoon of salt and some black pepper.

Pour the sauce into a container and keep in the fridge for a week. Or freeze it in portions. About 4 ladlefuls – roughly 350ml (12floz) – is enough for a straightforward sauce and I use this quantity in some recipes as a base for other sauces. Also freeze it in smaller portions of around 2 ladlefuls – about 175ml (6fl oz) – to add to recipes where I've specified a smaller amount.

Slow-roasted tomatoes

I love the benefits of slow roasting tomatoes. Slow cooking just intensifies that sweet yet tangy taste. You can use any tomatoes: plum, cherry or on the vine, just make sure they are ripe. Cut them in half or leave them whole – there are no hard and fast rules.

INGREDIENTS

12 plum tomatoes or a couple of vines of tomatoes or a couple of punnets of cherry tomatoes

4 tbsp balsamic vinegar

6 tbsp extra-virgin olive oil

1 tsp sugar

1 garlic clove, finely chopped

sea salt and pepper

2 tbsp chopped thyme

Here's how

Pre-heat the oven to 140°C/275°F/Gas Mark 1.

Lay the tomatoes on a baking tray, cut side up if you've halved them.

Mix together the vinegar, oil, sugar and garlic, and spoon a teaspoon of the mixture on to each tomato or tomato half. Sprinkle with sea salt, pepper and finally the thyme. Place them in the oven for an hour.

Store the tomatoes and their juices in a clean jam jar or container. They will keep in the fridge for a week or so. Chop and mix with pasta or try using them for a pizza base sauce – just spread them straight on to the dough.

Roasted garlic

Roasted garlic's got such an amazing flavour and is so versatile: you can just squeeze a bulb straight over hot pasta with a little olive oil and some Parmesan and dinner's ready. I even spread it on bread instead of butter!

INGREDIENTS

6 bulbs of garlic

2 sprigs of rosemary

2 sprigs of thyme

300ml (½ pint) vegetable oil

Here's how

Place the garlic, rosemary and thyme in a baking tray. Drizzle with 6 tbsp of oil and roast in the oven for 1 hour at 160°C/325°F/Gas Mark 3 until the garlic is soft and squidgy.

Leave to cool, then carefully transfer the bulbs into a large clean storage jar.

Pour the remaining oil over the top of the garlic until it is covered; this will help preserve it.

The garlic will keep in the fridge for at least 2–3 weeks, but to be honest once you've made this you will be using it for all sorts, so it will disappear in a flash. To use it, remove a bulb from the jar, pull the core out from the base of the bulb, then squeeze out all the sweet roast garlic flesh.

Preserved peppers

All it takes is a little time to preserve that wonderful sweet pepper taste. Slow roast them to bring back that beautiful flavour of the Med any time of year.

INGREDIENTS

6 red peppers

2 garlic cloves

100ml (3½fl oz) olive oil

salt and black pepper

sprig of rosemary

Here's how

Heat the oven to 160°C/325°F/Gas Mark 3. Place the peppers on a baking tray. Crush the garlic cloves, peel and add to the peppers.

Drizzle with the olive oil and season with plenty of salt, pepper and the rosemary. Roast the peppers for, say, 1 hour until really soft. Leave to cool.

Cut the tops off the peppers and pour off any liquid inside – even better, stand them upside down in a colander to drain. Throw the tops away.

Give the peppers a little squeeze, then place them in a clean storage jar. Add the garlic that you cooked with the peppers and pour over the oil they were cooked in. This will help preserve the peppers. If there isn't enough oil to cover them, top up with some extra-virgin olive oil.

The peppers should keep in the fridge for a few weeks and you can add them to all kinds of recipes.

Toasted walnuts

Whenever I buy walnuts, the first thing I do is toast them – it brings out the nutty flavour and you can really taste the difference when you cook with them.

INGREDIENTS

Walnuts

Olive oil

Here's how

Pre-heat the oven to 180°C/350°F/Gas Mark 4.

Place the walnuts on a roasting tray with 1 tbsp of olive oil and give them a good shake to coat them in the oil. Toast the nuts for 10 minutes until golden and crunchy. Cool then store in an airtight container for a week or so.

Toasted pine nuts

Pine nuts have a wonderful creamy texture to them. Follow this recipe and toast them and you will really taste the benefit – it will bring out their fabulous intense nutty flavour. Unlike toasted walnuts, above, there's no need to add oil when you toast them.

INGREDIENTS

Pine nuts

Here's how

Pre-heat the oven to 180°C/350°F/Gas Mark 4.

Put the pine nuts on a baking tray and toast them in the oven for 4–5 minutes until golden. Cool then store in an airtight container for a week or so.

Basic basil pesto

Pesto is my all-time desert-island ingredient. I love it spread on warm crusty bread or whipped into a little sour cream for a fabulous dip. Pesto is a great store-cupboard ingredient – it's so easy to make and so versatile. Serve any one of these with pasta for an instant supper.

INGREDIENTS

2 handfuls of basil

1 garlic clove, peeled

100g (3½oz) toasted pine nuts

75g (3oz) Parmesan or Pecorino

½ slice of soft white bread

juice of ½ lemon

100ml (3½fl oz) olive oil, plus extra to store

salt and pepper

Here's how

Place all the ingredients in a food processor and mix until smooth. Taste and adjust with a little extra lemon juice or some more salt and pepper if necessary. Pour the pesto into a clean jam jar or container. Smooth off the surface with a spoon, then cover with a film of olive oil to prevent any air coming in contact with the pesto. The pesto should keep in the fridge for a couple of weeks.

Instead of basil use:

Sage pesto 12 sage leaves and a handful of flat-leaf parsley
Mint pesto a handful each of mint leaves and flat-leaf parsley
Rocket pesto 250g (8oz) rocket and a handful of flat-leaf parsley
Sunblush tomato pesto 150g (5oz) sunblush tomatoes. Plus substitute 75g (3oz) toasted walnuts for pine nuts; add another garlic clove and use slightly less lemon juice – ¼ lemon rather than ½

Balsamic dressing

I've been making this dressing for as long as I can remember. It's got a great balance between the fruitiness of the vinegar and sweetness of the honey, all rounded off with a good olive oil. This dressing is as good on warm pasta as it is on a salad or freshly cooked new potatoes!

INGREDIENTS

100ml (3½fl oz) extra-virgin olive oil

100ml (3½fl oz) runny honey

100ml (3½fl oz) balsamic olive oil

Here's how

Place all the ingredients in a lidded container or jam jar and shake to mix together. Store in the fridge for up to 3 weeks.

Anchovy dressing

Fabulous on pasta, this dressing also goes really well with a tomato and mozzarella salad or is great drizzled over just-boiled new potatoes or a jacket potato instead of butter. Mmmm! Sounds yummy – I'm going to make some right now.

INGREDIENTS

4 salted anchovies

1 garlic clove

1 lemon

300ml (½ pint) extra-virgin olive oil

1 tbsp finely chopped rosemary

1 tsp cracked black peppercorns

Here's how

Place all the ingredients into a blender and process until smooth. Store in a clean jam jar or container.

Roasted lemon dressing

This dressing is great with pasta and it is really good just spooned over some nicely cooked fresh fish or chicken.

INGREDIENTS

2 lemons

100ml (3½fl oz) extra-virgin olive oil

1 tsp honey

salt and pepper

handful of flat-leaf parsley

sprig of rosemary (optional)

Here's how

Place a non-stick pan on a medium heat. Cut the lemons in half, rub a little oil on to the cut sides and place them cut side down in the pan. Cook the lemons until they take on a lovely golden colour.

Turn off the heat, carefully squeeze the lemon juice out into the pan and add the olive oil, honey, salt and pepper.

Finely chop the parsley and add to the dressing. Pour it into a clean jam jar or bottle and push in the sprig of rosemary if using. Store the dressing in the fridge – it will keep for 3–4 weeks at least.

Homemade ricotta cheese

Ricotta cheese is a great standby ingredient to have in the fridge. Use it in sweet and savoury dishes or simply serve it up with some deli pots of olives and antipasti and some warm ciabatta for an instant lunch or supper – just tuck in and enjoy.

INGREDIENTS

2.5 litres (4 pints) full fat milk

1 tsp salt

65ml (2½fl oz) lemon juice

Here's how

Heat the milk in a large pan. When it is just about to boil, remove it from the heat, add the salt and then the lemon juice. The mixture will instantly curdle; leave it on one side to cool for 20 minutes.

Pour the curd into a cheese mould or a sieve. Once the cheese is cool enough to handle it is ready to use.

Store-cupboard ingredients

I always have the following ingredients in my store cupboard and fridge, then I know I can put together something tasty for supper in minutes. Using flavour-packed ingredients like these can turn an ordinary dish into a special one.

anchovies	lemons
balsamic vinegar	nuts
capers	olives
chorizo sausage	pancetta or smoked streaky bacon
cracked black pepper	Parmesan or Pecorino cheese
dried chillies	pickled chillies
extra-virgin olive oil	salt
garlic	sun-dried tomatoes

Plus – absolutely essential – I have a selection of herbs growing in pots on the windowsill.

Spring

I love spring – it feels like everyone has come out to play after spending the winter inside pining to go out. For me one of the first signs of spring is spotting the new shoots of wild garlic in the hedgerows, when I take my daughter to see the lambs leaping around in the fields. Get out in the open air and, dare I say it, leave your big coat at home. And when you're back in the kitchen it's time to start livening up supper, with recipes bursting with spring flavours.

My five-minute spag bol

When there's no time to make a proper Bolognese sauce, follow my method and you can serve up that same great combination of flavours in minutes – using fresh pasta cuts the cooking time right down. Roasted tomatoes – see page 13 – are ideal but this dish works fine with fresh.

INGREDIENTS

500g (1lb) bag of fresh spaghetti

1 garlic clove

2 minute steaks, 125–150g (4–5oz) each

2 tbsp extra-virgin olive oil, plus extra to serve

sea salt and pepper

8 roasted tomatoes (see page 13) or a punnet of cherry tomatoes, halved

handful of basil leaves

Here's how

Bring a large pan of salted water to the boil. Meanwhile chop the garlic as finely as you can. Wrap your chopping board in a sheet of clingfilm – then you won't have to scrub it later – and lay the steaks on top. Drizzle them with olive oil, rub them with the chopped garlic, then season with plenty of sea salt and pepper.

Put a ridged grill pan over a medium heat.

Add the fresh spaghetti to the boiling water and cook for 3 minutes. Meanwhile lay the steaks in the grill pan and cook for 1 minute on each side. Remove the clingfilm from the chopping board and slice the cooked steaks into 1cm (½in) strips.

Drain the cooked pasta well, and tip it back into the pan. Add the steak and tomatoes. Tear up the basil leaves and add to the pan, along with salt, pepper and a drizzle of olive oil.

Wild garlic pesto

Wild garlic is one of nature's free gifts and one of my favourite treats in spring. Make the most of its short season and try this easy pesto recipe. If you like it, why not double up the recipe next time and leave a tub in the fridge? (It will keep for a couple of weeks.) Use it on pizza, sandwiches and salads; stir it into stews or mashed potato, or spread it on chicken breasts before baking. If you can't get wild garlic, use a mixture of rocket and spinach instead: two good-sized handfuls of rocket and a handful of baby spinach will do it.

INGREDIENTS

400g (13oz) spaghetti

100g (3½oz) walnuts

2 good-sized handfuls of wild garlic, washed

handful of parsley

1 garlic clove, peeled

100ml (3½fl oz) olive oil, plus extra to serve

1 slice of white bread, broken into pieces

100g (3½oz) Parmesan or Pecorino, grated, plus extra to serve

squeeze of lemon juice

salt and pepper

punnet of cherry tomatoes, cut in half, to serve

2 handfuls of wild rocket leaves, to serve

extra-virgin olive oil, to serve

2 tbsp pine nuts, to serve

Here's how

Cook the spaghetti in a large pan of boiling salted water.

While the pasta is cooking, heat the oven to 180°C/350°F/Gas Mark 4. Place the walnuts on a roasting tray and cook for 6 minutes until crunchy. Leave to cool.

Put the wild garlic, parsley, garlic clove, olive oil and bread in a food processor and blend until smooth. Add the walnuts and grated cheese and blend again.

Taste the pesto and if you feel it needs sharpening up, add a little lemon juice and season with a little salt and pepper.

Drain the cooked spaghetti in a large colander, then tip it back into the pan. Add a few spoonfuls of pesto, the cherry tomatoes and rocket.

Serve with a little more grated cheese and a drizzle of extra-virgin olive oil and scatter with pine nuts.

Roasted gnocchi with lemon & rosemary

Gnocchi make a nice change from potatoes. Try serving them up with a piece of grilled chicken or steamed fish instead of mash or chips. To turn this into an all-in-one dish, add some cooked chicken or leftover roasted vegetables to the frying pan when you add the gnocchi.

INGREDIENTS

375g (12oz) readymade gnocchi

2 tbsp olive oil

1 garlic clove

1 tbsp chopped rosemary

zest and juice of 1 lemon

salt and pepper

Here's how

Cook the gnocchi in a large pan of boiling salted water. When they start to float to the surface, they are cooked.

Drain the gnocchi in a colander until dry.

Heat a non-stick frying pan. Drizzle the gnocchi with olive oil then tip them into the hot frying pan. Chop the garlic finely and add to the pan with the rosemary. When the gnocchi are golden and crisp, remove from the heat and add the lemon zest and juice, and season.

Olives, anchovies & capers

This is one of my favourite pizza toppings, so I came up with a simple way to transfer the flavours to a bowl of pasta. The saltiness of the anchovies melts into the pasta and balances the sweetness of the tomatoes, to make a great quick supper.

INGREDIENTS

375g (12oz) pasta

5–6 fresh plum tomatoes, quartered

16 pitted black olives

2 tbsp mini capers

6–8 salted anchovies

2 tbsp extra-virgin olive oil

salt and pepper

handful of basil leaves, chopped

anchovy dressing (see page 18)

Here's how

Cook the pasta in a large pan of boiling salted water.

Tip the cooked pasta into a colander and stand it in the sink to drain.

Put the tomatoes into the pasta saucepan with the olives, capers and anchovies and heat through.

Put the pasta back in the pan, drizzle with olive oil and season. Add the chopped basil to the pan. Stir to mix, adding a dash of homemade anchovy dressing to finish the dish, then serve.

Spring cabbage & pancetta

There's something about cabbage and bacon – it's a match made in heaven. Putting white wine into the equation helps bring out the flavours. I often make this dish on a Monday evening, when I'll add in any leftover chicken from Sunday lunch too.

INGREDIENTS

375g (12oz) fusilli

100g (3½oz) rashers of pancetta, diced (or use ready prepared)

2–3 tbsp olive oil

half a spring cabbage

100ml (3½fl oz) dry white wine

salt and pepper

Here's how

Cook the pasta in a large pan of boiling salted water.

While the pasta is cooking, set a deep non-stick frying pan over a medium heat. Add the diced pancetta with the olive oil and fry until it starts to caramelise, stirring and shaking the pan from time to time. Using a large sharp knife, slice the cabbage as thinly as possible and add to the pan.

Pour in the wine and turn up the heat. Cook until the liquid has almost disappeared – about 5–6 minutes. Drain the cooked pasta and add to the cabbage. Season with salt and pepper and serve.

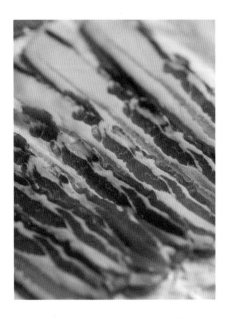

Spaghetti frittata

I'm a professional chef yet somehow I still end up cooking too much pasta. This recipe is a great way of using up leftover spaghetti. It has to be spaghetti – hollow shapes like penne don't allow the egg to cook properly. This frittata is one of my wife's favourite comfort foods.

INGREDIENTS

2 large eggs

1 red chilli

1 tbsp homemade basil pesto (see page 17)

50g (2oz) Parmesan

50g (2oz) cooked spaghetti

1 tbsp olive oil

Here's how

Crack the eggs into a mixing bowl and whisk together. Deseed the red chilli and chop finely and add to the eggs, followed by the pesto. Finely grate the Parmesan and add it to the mixture.

Add the cooked spaghetti and mix together to ensure the pasta gets covered in the egg mixture.

Heat a non-stick frying pan and add the olive oil. Pour the mixture into the pan and cook gently on both sides for 4–5 minutes until firm. Turn the frittata by putting a plate over the pan and turning the pan upside down. Slide the frittata back into the pan and cook the other side.

Cut into portions and serve.

Black olives with roasted garlic

For years I didn't eat olives. Then I don't know how it happened, but when I turned 30, I found an olive I liked – a rich black Kalamata. There is an olive out there for everyone: use your favourite to make this recipe. Add some chopped fresh chilli if you want to give it a kick.

INGREDIENTS

375g (12oz) pasta

250g (8oz) pitted black olives, or green if you prefer

2 tbsp pine nuts

4–5 tbsp olive oil

handful of flat-leaf parsley, chopped

1 bulb of roasted garlic (see page 14)

salt and pepper

grated Parmesan, to serve (optional)

Here's how

Cook the pasta in a large pan of boiling salted water.

Tip the cooked pasta into a colander and stand it in the sink to drain.

While the pasta is draining, place the pitted black olives, pine nuts, olive oil and chopped parsley into the pasta pan on a low heat. Pull the core out from the base of the garlic bulb and squeeze out the cloves into the pan. Then add the cooked pasta. Stir together and season with black pepper.

Finish with a little grated Parmesan, if you like.

Pancetta & roasted garlic

This is a great way of combining roasted garlic with the salty smoky flavour of pancetta. It's quick, easy and it tastes great. Roasting garlic takes away that harsh raw taste and makes it a lot smoother and very sweet.

INGREDIENTS

375g (12oz) pasta

200g (7oz) rashers of pancetta (or use ready diced)

1–2 bulbs of roasted garlic (see page 14)

2 tbsp ricotta

handful of flat-leaf parsley, chopped

salt and pepper

100g (3½oz) Parmesan, grated

Here's how

Cook the pasta in a large pan of boiling salted water.

While the pasta is cooking, dice the pancetta. Place a non-stick pan on a medium heat. Add the pancetta and cook for about 5 minutes. Remove a bulb or two of roasted garlic from the jar of oil. Pull the core out from the base of the bulb, then squeeze out all the sweet roast garlic into the pan. Stir in the ricotta.

Drain the cooked pasta and add to the garlic, pancetta and ricotta. Stir the pasta to make sure it is coated.

Add the chopped parsley, season and top with grated Parmesan.

Purple sprouting broccoli with anchovy, lemon & garlic

When you start to see tender stems of purple sprouting broccoli for sale, it means spring is here. That can only be a good thing – lighter evenings and no more defrosting the car of a morning. It might even be warm enough to sit outside and eat!

INGREDIENTS

375g (12oz) pasta

2 x 200g (7oz) packs purple sprouting broccoli

1 garlic clove

1 quantity roasted lemon dressing (see page 19)

3 tbsp toasted pine nuts (see page 16)

6 anchovies

salt and pepper

Here's how

Cook the pasta in a large pan of boiling salted water.

Meanwhile snap the broccoli in half and add it to the pasta after it has been cooking for 5 minutes. Crush the garlic. Tip the cooked pasta and broccoli into a colander and stand it in the sink to drain.

Pour the dressing into the pan you have just cooked the pasta in, followed by the pine nuts, anchovies and crushed garlic.

Add the pasta and broccoli, and stir carefully so that all the pasta is coated in the dressing.

Taste and season with a little black pepper. You don't need any more salt as the anchovies are salted and there was salt in the cooking water.

Spring greens & rocket

When spring greens are fresh and in season, you don't want to do much to them. Pan frying them off a little and adding pasta is a great way to appreciate their freshness, without losing their fresh, crisp, crunchy taste of spring.

INGREDIENTS

375g (12oz) pasta

1 garlic clove

1 tbsp chopped rosemary

50g (2oz) butter

4 spring onions

¼ head of spring greens

squeeze of lemon juice

salt and pepper

handful of rocket, to serve

extra-virgin olive oil, to serve

Here's how

Cook the pasta in a large pan of boiling salted water.

While the pasta is cooking, crush and chop the garlic. Heat a frying pan on a medium heat, then add the garlic, rosemary and butter, and cook for about 1 minute. Roughly chop the spring onions and spring greens, then add to the pan and cook for 5–6 minutes until gently wilted.

Drain the cooked pasta and stir into the greens. Add a squeeze of lemon and season with salt and pepper. Serve scattered with rocket and a drizzle of extra-virgin olive oil.

Lemon & baby spinach pesto

A quick, light and fresh-tasting dish that's perfect for a fast supper or for a packed lunch to take to work or to send the kids off to school with – or even to take on an early picnic. Pack the cooled pasta in a suitable container and keep in the fridge until needed.

INGREDIENTS

375g (12oz) pasta

500g (1lb) bag of baby spinach

2 garlic cloves, peeled

75g (3oz) pine nuts

juice of 1 lemon

100g (3½oz) Parmesan, grated

1 slice of bread

3 tbsp extra-virgin olive oil

salt and pepper

Here's how

Cook the pasta in a large pan of boiling salted water.

While the pasta is cooking, make the pesto. Put all the ingredients in a food processor and blend together. Taste the pesto and adjust the flavour by adding more garlic, seasoning or lemon juice if you like.

Drain the cooked pasta, return it to the pan and stir through a few tablespoons of pesto.

Kids' spag bol with five hidden vegetables

Most kids love Bolognese, so why not get sneaky and hide a few extra portions of vegetables in the sauce? When we were small, my brother and I would fish out all the chopped mushrooms, sliced celery and chunks of carrot, and line them up along the edge of our plates. Use my method and the kids will never find them.

INGREDIENTS

1 medium onion

2 carrots

10 mushrooms

4 celery sticks

2 courgettes

3 garlic cloves

3 tbsp olive oil

875g (1¾lb) minced beef

½ glass red wine

4 sun-dried tomatoes

2 x 400g (13oz) cans chopped tomatoes

1 tbsp Worcestershire sauce

1 beef stock cube

1 tbsp dried Italian herbs

1 tsp sugar

salt and pepper

375g (12oz) spaghetti

Here's how

Peel and chop the veg into chunks, place them in a food processor and blend into tiny pieces. You may need to do this in batches.

Place a medium saucepan on the heat and add the olive oil. Add the vegetable pieces and cook for 5–10 minutes until soft. Add the minced beef. Use a wooden spoon to break up the mince and cook until brown. Add the red wine.

Using scissors, snip the sun-dried tomatoes into little pieces straight into the pan.

Add the canned tomatoes, Worcestershire sauce, stock cube, herbs and sugar. Season with salt and pepper. Leave the pan on a gentle heat to simmer for 30–40 minutes.

After about 25 minutes cook the spaghetti in a large pan of boiling salted water. Drain the cooked pasta and serve with the Bolognese sauce.

Baby spinach & smoked salmon

You can buy some really good smoked salmon these days. If you've bought the very best, the key is not to do too much to it – so make sure you add the salmon at the very last minute, to savour that fabulous smoky flavour.

INGREDIENTS

375g (12oz) pasta

140g (4¾oz) baby spinach

150g (5oz) smoked salmon

zest and juice of ½ lemon

3 tbsp extra-virgin olive oil

salt and pepper

Here's how

Cook the pasta in a large pan of boiling salted water.

While the pasta is cooking, either chop finely or tear up the baby spinach leaves. Slice the smoked salmon: roll it up first then cut across in strips ½cm (1in) wide. Leave it on the chopping board, ready to add to the pasta with the spinach.

Tip the cooked pasta into a colander and stand it in the sink to drain. Return the pan to the heat, add the lemon zest and the juice, followed by the olive oil. Add the spinach, followed by the pasta. Season with a little salt and plenty of freshly ground black pepper. Give it a good mix, so all the pasta gets a generous coating of the dressing. Finally add the star of the show, the smoked salmon, and give the pasta one last stir before serving.

Baby spinach & ricotta easy cannelloni

I always serve up this dish when I have meat-eaters and vegetarians round for dinner – it seems to go down well with both parties. The creaminess of the ricotta works perfectly in this recipe but, I have to admit, I'm a sucker for the crispy bits!

INGREDIENTS

1kg (2lb) spinach

300g (10oz) homemade ricotta cheese (see page 20)

2 egg yolks

150g (5oz) Parmesan, grated

4 tbsp toasted pine nuts (see page 16)

nutmeg

salt and pepper

For the white sauce

50g (2oz) butter

50g (2oz) plain flour

600ml (1 pint) milk

12 fresh lasagne sheets

2 ladlefuls – about 175ml (6fl oz) – basic tomato sauce (see page 12)

75g (3oz) breadcrumbs

olive oil, for drizzling

Here's how

Heat a large pan and add the spinach with a sprinkle of salt and pepper, and just a splash (max 2 tbsp) of water – all you need is to create a little steam to cook the spinach.

After about 4–5 minutes the spinach will wilt and darken. Turn off the heat and leave to cool. You should have around 500g (1lb) cooked spinach.

Scoop the ricotta into a mixing bowl and add the egg yolks, half the grated Parmesan, the pine nuts and a few rasps of grated nutmeg, just to give a little flavour. Mix together and season with a little salt and plenty of black pepper.

When the spinach is cooled, squeeze out as much water as you possibly can using your hands – you will get more out of it than you think. Place the spinach on a chopping board, chop it up using a large knife, then add to the ricotta mixture.

Make a white sauce: melt the butter in a pan, add the flour and mix together to form a paste. Stir the mixture for a minute or so, to cook the flour so it will thicken without leaving a floury taste. Add the milk a little at a time and mix. I find a whisk works best for this job. Cook the sauce on a medium heat, stirring, until it thickens. Season with a little salt and pepper, then leave to stand until you are ready.

Heat the oven to 180°C/350°F/Gas Mark 4.

Lay out all the sheets of fresh lasagne on a chopping board. If you don't have enough space, do this part in two stages. You're going to roll up the lasagne sheets round the filling to form the cannelloni.

Place 1 ladleful of the tomato sauce in the bottom of an ovenproof dish, then divide the remaining sauce between the sheets of pasta. Then add the ricotta and spinach filling, shaping the filling across the shortest side of the sheet in a sausage shape. Roll the pasta up around the filling just like a sausage roll.

Place the rolled up pasta tubes in the ovenproof dish. Pour over the white sauce and top with the remaining Parmesan and breadcrumbs. Drizzle with a little olive oil to help get those breadcrumbs really crispy, then bake in the oven for 40 minutes until golden.

Dried porcini & tomato ragu

Porcini mushrooms are fantastic when they are in season; they have an amazingly earthy and meaty flavour – the drawback is their price. Keep a look out for sliced dry porcini: they are lots cheaper and the drying process intensifies their flavour, which will give this dish a boost.

INGREDIENTS

100g (3½oz) dried porcini mushrooms

375g (12oz) spaghetti

4 ladlefuls – about 350ml (12fl oz) – basic tomato sauce (see page 12)

1 bulb roasted garlic (see page 14)

1 tbsp chopped rosemary

salt and pepper

75g (3oz) Parmesan, grated

flat-leaf parsley, chopped

Here's how

Boil the kettle, place the dried mushrooms in a bowl and cover with boiling water. Leave to stand for 5–10 minutes to rehydrate.

Cook the pasta in a large pan of boiling salted water. While the pasta is cooking, pour the tomato sauce into a medium pan and warm gently. Remove the roasted garlic from the jar and squeeze out any excess oil. Pull the core out from the base of the bulb, then squeeze all the roast garlic into the pan. Add the chopped rosemary and bring the sauce to a simmer.

Lift the mushrooms from the water – don't throw the water away – squeeze them out and chop them roughly, then add to the sauce. The water that the mushrooms were soaking in is packed full of flavour, so pour it carefully into the sauce. Leave the last few tablespoons behind so that any gritty bits in the bottom of the bowl don't end up in the pan.

Taste the sauce and season with a little salt and pepper if required.

When the pasta is cooked, drain it in a colander, then add to the sauce. Give it a good stir and serve, topped with grated Parmesan and parsley.

Spring lamb pastichio

I have great memories of eating this dish on holiday with my parents in Greece. Yes, that's right, I said Greece – not all pasta is Italian, you know. My version of this recipe combines ideas from two of my favourite culinary nations.

INGREDIENTS

375g (12oz) macaroni

For the white sauce

50g (2oz) butter

50g (2oz) flour

600ml (1 pint) milk

For the lamb mixture

1 medium white onion

2 carrots

3 garlic cloves

1 tbsp olive oil

1 tbsp chopped rosemary

2 juniper berries

½ cinnamon stick

1 small aubergine

625g (1¼lb) minced lamb

2 x 400g (13oz) cans chopped tomatoes

1 beef or vegetable stock cube

salt and pepper

For the topping

100g (3½oz) Cheddar, grated

Here's how

Pre-heat the oven to 180°C/350°F/Gas Mark 4.

Cook the pasta in a large pan of boiling salted water.

While the pasta is cooking, make the white sauce. Place a medium pan on the heat and melt the butter. Add the flour and stir for a minute with a wooden spoon so that it cooks and you are not left with a floury-tasting sauce. Change over to a whisk and start whisking in the milk a little at a time. Keep whisking until the sauce is smooth and has thickened up – it should be thick enough to coat the back of a spoon.

By the time the sauce is finished, the pasta should be cooked. Drain the pasta and return it to the pan. Pour the white sauce over the pasta, give it a stir and put the pan to one side.

Chop the onion, carrots and garlic. Place another pan on the heat. Pour the olive oil in the pan and add the chopped vegetables and the rosemary.

Squash the juniper berries and snap the cinnamon stick, and add to the pan. Chop the aubergine into 1cm (½in) cubes and add to the pan.

Add the minced lamb and cook for 5 minutes until the meat has browned. Pour in the canned tomatoes and pop in the stock cube. Let everything simmer for 20–30 minutes.

Leave the lid off the pan so that the liquid reduces a little, as this will intensify the flavours and make a better-tasting dish.

When the mince is cooked, have a little taste and season with salt and pepper if required.

Remove the cinnamon stick and spoon the mince into an ovenproof dish. Top with the pasta, spreading it over to cover the mince. Top with grated cheese and bake in the oven for 45 minutes until it's all golden and crispy.

I like to serve this dish with a big Greek salad and some warm pitta bread.

Puttanesca pasta

Puttanesca is one of my favourite Italian flavour combinations. I just love capers, olives and anchovies and they are always in my store cupboard, so I can rustle this dish up anytime – if you haven't got fresh tomatoes, improvise and use drained canned ones instead.

INGREDIENTS

375g (12oz) pasta

6 salted anchovies

1 garlic clove

punnet of cherry tomatoes, halved

2 tbsp capers

handful of basil leaves, chopped

freshly ground black pepper

handful of black olives

Here's how

Cook the pasta in a large pan of boiling salted water.

While the pasta is cooking, chop the anchovies and garlic really finely so that they almost become a paste.

Tip the cooked pasta into a colander and stand it in the sink to drain.

Add the chopped anchovies and garlic to the pasta pan with the tomatoes and capers and warm over a medium heat. Return the pasta to the pan and stir to mix. Stir in the basil, season with black pepper and serve with black olives on the side.

Watercress, Taleggio & black pepper

Watercress has a wonderful peppery kick to it that really stands up to the rich creaminess of the Taleggio cheese, which is a little like Brie – I love it! No sauce needed for this dish, as the cheese will melt over the pasta to create a sauce all of its own.

INGREDIENTS

375g (12oz) pasta

2 bunches of watercress

150g (5oz) Taleggio

3 tbsp cream

squeeze of lemon juice

2 tbsp extra-virgin olive oil

salt and pepper

Here's how

Cook the pasta in a large pan of boiling salted water.

While the pasta is cooking, pick off the main leaves from the stems of watercress. Discard the stems and chop the leaves. Dice the cheese into 1cm (½ in) cubes.

Tip the cooked pasta into a colander and stand it in the sink to drain. Add the watercress and cheese to the pasta pan, followed by the cream and drained pasta. Add a squeeze of lemon juice to cut through the creaminess. Stir in the olive oil and season with plenty of black pepper.

Sausages with tomatoes & cream

This recipe was given to me by a great friend of mine: he is a strong-willed northern Italian and passionate about food – luckily he loves my cooking! So I cook for him and he teaches me the art of fly fishing, which seems like a fair deal to me.

INGREDIENTS

375g (12oz) penne pasta

½ onion

2 garlic cloves

2 tbsp olive oil

6 sausages

400g (13oz) can chopped tomatoes

salt and pepper

75ml (3fl oz) double cream

a few basil leaves, chopped

Here's how

Cook the pasta in a large pan of boiling salted water.

While the pasta is cooking, chop the onion and garlic finely. Place a non-stick frying pan on a medium heat. Add the onion and garlic to the frying pan with the olive oil. While the onions soften, cut off and discard the skin from the sausages. Put the sausages in the pan and stir with a wooden spoon, breaking them up into little pieces.

After they have cooked for 2–3 minutes, add the can of chopped tomatoes and season with salt and pepper. Turn up the heat until the sauce comes to the boil, then turn it down and let it simmer for 10–15 minutes – it should reduce by half approximately.

Stir in the double cream. Drain the cooked pasta and add to the pan. Give it a good stir.

Serve with a little chopped basil and an extra twist of black pepper.

Summer

This is it, the great British summer. Enjoy it while it lasts – blink and you may miss it! Summer for me represents all kinds of cooking opportunities. Every chance I get, I want to eat outside: dinner, lunch or breakfast, food always tastes better in the open air. If you're a keen veg grower, you'll be enjoying the fruits of your garden labours; if not, you'll be buying and enjoying the fruits of someone else's. Whichever's the case, try to lighten up a little in the kitchen – less is, more often than not, more at this time of year. So if you've got some amazing seasonal vegetables, do a little less to them than you normally would – and let the true taste of summer come through.

Fennel & tomato pesto

I love pesto, but at first all I could find were recipes for basil pesto. So I started to experiment with all kinds of different flavours. This is one of my favourites. Tomato and fennel really work together: the fennel seems to add a lightness to the pesto that balances all the flavours.

INGREDIENTS

375g (12oz) pasta

1 fennel bulb

200g (7oz) sunblush tomatoes

1 tbsp fennel seeds, plus extra
   to serve

2 garlic cloves, peeled

100ml (3½fl oz) olive oil

75g (3oz) Parmesan, grated

juice of ½ lemon

25ml (1fl oz) aniseed liqueur
   (optional – if you've got some
   lurking in the back of your
   cupboard, add a splash)

salt and pepper

Here's how

Cook the pasta in a large pan of boiling salted water.

While the pasta is cooking, chop the fennel into small pieces, reserving a few fronds to add before serving. Place in a saucepan on a medium heat with 200ml (7fl oz) water and simmer until the fennel is soft. Strain off the water and leave the fennel to cool.

Blend the fennel and the rest of the ingredients in a food processor until smooth. Have a taste and season if required. If the pesto is quite rich, add an extra squeeze of lemon juice just to balance the flavours.

Drain the cooked pasta, return it to the pan, stir through the pesto and serve, scattered with the reserved fronds and a few extra fennel seeds.

Asparagus & Pecorino

This is one of my wife Emma's favourite dishes. We always make it as soon as great British asparagus goes on sale in the shops. By the way, don't throw away the bases of the spears – you can use them to make soup another day.

INGREDIENTS

375g (12oz) spaghetti

2 bunches of asparagus

100g (3½oz) mascarpone cheese

100g (3½oz) Pecorino cheese, grated

1 tsp thyme leaves

squeeze of lemon juice

salt and pepper

2 tbsp pine nuts

Here's how

Cook the spaghetti in a large pan of boiling salted water. Snap the asparagus at a point where they break easily – usually about halfway down. After the pasta has been cooking for 5 minutes add the asparagus spear ends to the pan.

Tip the cooked spaghetti and asparagus into a colander and stand them in the sink to drain. Return the pasta pan to the heat and add the mascarpone and grated Pecorino, reserving a little Pecorino to sprinkle on the finished dish. Heat them until they melt. Stir in the thyme. Season with a squeeze of lemon juice and some salt and pepper.

Stir in the asparagus and pasta using a wooden spoon, then serve, sprinkled with the remaining Pecorino and the pine nuts.

Peas & Parmesan

The first British peas on sale are a sure sign that summer is here. Make the most of them with this simple recipe. The sweetness of the peas works really well with the saltiness of the cheese. This dish can be enjoyed hot or serve it cold as a salad instead.

INGREDIENTS

375g (12oz) farfalle pasta

250g (8oz) garden peas or frozen petits pois

1 small onion

2 tbsp olive oil

200g (7oz) tub of crème fraîche with chives and onion

finely grated zest of 1 lemon

3 tbsp finely grated Parmesan

salt and pepper

1 tbsp chopped flat-leaf parsley

Here's how

Cook the pasta in a large pan of boiling salted water. Add the peas for the last 2–3 minutes.

While the pasta is cooking, chop the onion finely. Heat the olive oil in a saucepan and fry the onion gently until softened and cooked, but not brown. Stir in the crème fraîche and warm it through, adding 3 tbsp of the pasta cooking water to thin it down. Now stir in the lemon zest and 2 tbsp of the Parmesan.

Drain the pasta and peas really well, add them to the sauce and stir gently. Season with salt and pepper. Serve sprinkled with the parsley and the remaining Parmesan.

Roasted tomatoes, pine nuts & torn basil

Slow-roasted tomatoes are intensely sweet yet tangy. I always keep some handy in my fridge. This is one occasion where less is more: when the tomatoes taste this good, there's nothing more needed – except maybe a handful of basil and some pine nuts.

INGREDIENTS

375g (12oz) conchiglie pasta

12 roasted cherry tomatoes (see page 13)

salt and pepper

3 tbsp toasted pine nuts (see page 16)

handful of basil

extra-virgin olive oil

Here's how

Cook the pasta in a large pan of boiling salted water.

Drain the cooked pasta thoroughly in a colander, then tip it back into the pan.

Add the tomatoes, a little black pepper and the pine nuts. Mix together to break up the tomatoes and coat the pasta. Serve with plenty of freshly torn basil and a drizzle of good extra-virgin olive oil.

Roasted summer vegetables

This recipe is a simple celebration of all that's great in the garden or the vegetable patch right now. When you roast vegetables it brings out all their natural sweetness and makes them incredibly more-ish.

INGREDIENTS

375g (12oz) pasta

1 garlic clove

2 tbsp olive oil

bunch of spring onions

2 courgettes

2 red peppers

punnet of cherry tomatoes, halved

1 tsp chopped fresh rosemary

4 sage leaves, chopped

splash of white wine

125g (4oz) ball of mozzarella

salt and pepper

handful of basil

handful of black olives

extra-virgin olive oil, to serve

Here's how

Cook the pasta in a large pan of boiling salted water.

While the pasta is cooking, crush and chop the garlic. Heat a non-stick frying pan and add the olive oil and garlic. Slice the spring onions, courgettes and peppers, and add to the pan, followed by the cherry tomatoes. Add the herbs to the pan. Add the white wine and cook until the liquid almost disappears.

Drain the cooked pasta in a colander and add to the vegetables.

Finally cut the mozzarella into pieces and add them to the pasta followed by a seasoning of salt and black pepper, basil leaves, olives and a drizzle of extra-virgin olive oil.

Radicchio & sweet garlic

Radicchio is a really under-used vegetable in the UK. However, in Italy they use loads of it: it's got a pleasantly bitter taste that contrasts really well with the sweetness of the roasted garlic in this dish. The bacon adds another dimension, but you can leave it out for a veggie version.

INGREDIENTS

375g (12oz) pasta

2 heads of radicchio

4 tbsp extra-virgin olive oil (or use a little of the oil from the roasted garlic, below)

25g (1oz) butter

4 rashers of smoked bacon, chopped

sprig of rosemary, leaves stripped and chopped

salt and pepper

2 bulbs of roasted garlic (see page 14)

2 tbsp balsamic vinegar

chopped flat-leaf parsley, to serve

grated Pecorino, to serve

Here's how

Cook the pasta in a large pan of boiling salted water.

While the pasta is cooking, cut the radicchio into quarters then cut out and discard the white core. Chop the radicchio into 1cm (½in) wide pieces.

Tip the cooked pasta into a colander and stand it in the sink to drain. Put the pasta pan on a medium heat, add the olive oil and butter, followed by the radicchio and bacon. Cook for a few minutes to soften. Add the chopped rosemary and season with salt and pepper.

Take the roasted garlic bulbs out of the jar of oil. Pull the core out from the base of each bulb and squeeze out the cloves into the pan. Add the balsamic vinegar and give everything a good stir around to break up the garlic – it will become almost like a sauce.

Add the drained pasta and mix together to coat the pasta. Serve scattered with chopped flat-leaf parsley and grated Pecorino.

Courgette farfalle

This quick and easy dish is a good way of using up courgettes – and it's so simple. In my experience it's also a good way to get the kids eating a vegetable they might usually turn their nose up at: grating courgettes is one method of disguising them.

INGREDIENTS

375g (12oz) farfalle pasta

1 garlic clove

2 tbsp extra-virgin olive oil

4 courgettes

1 tbsp chopped rosemary

1 tbsp chopped thyme

100g (3½oz) Parmesan, finely grated

salt and pepper

Here's how

Cook the pasta in a large pan of boiling salted water.

While the pasta is cooking, chop the garlic finely. Place a non-stick pan on a medium heat. Add the garlic and olive oil. Grate the courgettes straight into the pan and cook for 3–4 minutes. Add the chopped herbs.

When the pasta is cooked, drain it well and add to the courgettes. Stir to mix, add the Parmesan and season with a little black pepper.

Seafood parcels with herbs & Pernod

This recipe is a great way to use up leftover pasta. It's also a brilliant dinner party dish, because all the work is done in advance – leaving you plenty of time to enjoy yourself. That's the way a dinner party should be.

INGREDIENTS

175g (6oz) leftover cooked pasta per person or 375g (12oz) dried pasta

200g (7oz) salmon fillet

200g (7oz) seabass fillet

2 mackerel fillets

8 tiger prawns

4 ladlefuls – about 350ml (12fl oz) – basic tomato sauce (see page 12)

2 tbsp Pernod or any aniseed-flavour alcohol

1 garlic clove, chopped

handful of flat-leaf parsley, chopped

salt and pepper

lemon juice

Here's how

If you haven't got any leftover pasta, start by cooking the dried pasta. Once it is cooked, drain it in a colander and run it under the cold tap to stop it cooking further.

Cut the fish fillets into 2cm (¾in) chunks. It's really important that they are all the same size so that they all cook at the same rate.

Place the fish chunks in a mixing bowl and add the prawns, basic tomato sauce, alcohol, chopped garlic and half the chopped parsley. Add the cooked pasta and mix together so all the pasta gets coated. Season with a little salt and pepper.

Pre-heat the oven to 180°C/350°F/Gas Mark 4.

Cut 8 pieces of kitchen foil, 30cm (12in) square. Use 2 pieces for each parcel to make a double layer of foil. Divide the pasta and seafood mixture between the foil, placing it in the centre. Fold the foil in half and seal up all the edges.

Place the foil parcels on a baking tray and cook for 20 minutes. You can tell when the fish is ready as the parcels will puff up with all the steam inside.

When you're ready to serve, tear open the parcels and finish with the last of the parsley and a good squeeze of lemon juice.

Courgette, chilli & mint salad

This is a fresh-tasting salad with a cheeky kick from the chilli. This dish will be a welcome addition to any good barbecue or picnic and, if you've made up a bottle of my roasted lemon dressing on page 19, you can rustle it up in minutes once the pasta and courgettes are cooked.

INGREDIENTS

375g (12oz) pasta

3 courgettes

1 quantity roasted lemon dressing (see page 19)

salt and pepper

2 handfuls of fresh mint

1 red chilli, deseeded and diced

Here's how

Start cooking the pasta in a large pan of boiling salted water. After 8 minutes grate the courgettes straight into the pan with the pasta and continue to cook for a further 5 minutes.

Drain the cooked pasta and courgettes in a colander, then return them to the pan.

Pour the roasted lemon dressing over the warm pasta, season with salt and pepper and leave the pasta to cool.

To serve add lots of chopped mint and a scatter of diced red chilli.

Nutty pasta

This is a dish I came across in southern Italy. I was surprised just how fantastic the pasta tasted when it was mixed with some crunchy seasonal nuts. It just goes to show you don't always have to top pasta with cheese.

INGREDIENTS

375g (12oz) pasta

50g (2oz) walnuts

50g (2oz) pistachios

50g (2oz) pine nuts

2 tbsp extra-virgin olive oil

salt and pepper

1 tsp honey

1 garlic clove, chopped

handful of flat-leaf parsley, chopped

300g (10oz) tub mascarpone cheese

squeeze of lemon juice

4 sage leaves

75g (3oz) Pecorino, grated, to serve

Here's how

Cook the pasta in a large pan of boiling salted water.

While the pasta is cooking, place a non-stick pan on a medium heat. Add the nuts, along with the olive oil and cook them for 3–4 minutes. Don't leave the pan – the nuts can turn from golden to black in a matter of seconds. As soon as the nuts are cooked, take them off the heat and season with salt and the honey.

Tip the cooked pasta into a colander and stand it in the sink to drain.

Put the chopped garlic, parsley and mascarpone in the pasta pan with a squeeze of lemon juice. Season with a little salt and black pepper, then stir in the pasta. To serve, scatter the nuts over the pasta and use scissors to snip the sage leaves over the top. Finish with grated Pecorino.

Blackened chilli, basil & lemon

Charring the chillies before using them mellows the heat without losing the flavour – a good tip for anyone who likes chilli but not the full-on lip-numbing experience. Just remember the green chillies are usually a lot hotter than the red ones!

INGREDIENTS

375g (12oz) pasta

2 chillies

1 garlic clove

handful of basil

4 tbsp extra-virgin olive oil

zest and juice of 1 lemon

salt and pepper

Here's how

Cook the pasta in a large pan of boiling salted water.

While the pasta is cooking, char the chillies. Turn a gas hob to medium heat. Spear the chillies on the end of a fork and carefully sit them in the hob flame until they blacken. As long as the chillies are in the flame and not the fork, the fork won't get hot. Turn the fork from time to time to char the chillies evenly. (If you don't have a gas hob, grill the chillies until the skin blisters and blackens.) Leave them on a chopping board to cool.

Chop the garlic and tear up the basil. Chop and deseed the cooled chillies.

Tip the cooked pasta into a colander and stand it in the sink to drain. Add the olive oil to the pasta pan with the chopped garlic and cook on a medium heat for 1 minute. Put the pasta back in the pan, followed by the lemon zest and juice. Season with salt and pepper. Finally add the chilli and plenty of torn up basil.

BBQ chicken & sunblush tomatoes

When you have a weekend barbecue, make sure you cook a little extra chicken just for this recipe – then you can put a quick supper together on Monday. If you haven't got any leftover chicken you can always cook some specially – use boneless thighs, season them with salt, pepper and lemon zest and roast for 35 minutes at 180˚C/350˚F/Gas Mark 4.

INGREDIENTS

375g (12oz) pasta

1 quantity roasted lemon dressing (see page 19)

4 barbecued chicken thighs

100g (3½oz) sunblush tomatoes

handful of basil, roughly chopped

salt and pepper

Here's how

Cook the pasta in a large pan of boiling salted water.

While the pasta is cooking, pour the roasted lemon dressing into a pan and place on a low heat. Tear the chicken into small pieces and add to the pan with the sunblush tomatoes, and warm through for 2–3 minutes.

Drain the cooked pasta and add to the pan with the chopped basil. Stir the pasta so that it is evenly coated with the dressing. Season with salt and pepper, then serve.

Risoni salad with lemon, mint & feta

A light and fragrant pasta salad perfect for serving on hot days. To me, it's like a summer garden on a plate – just what you want when the weather is warm. Remember that risoni pasta is so small, it's best to drain it in a sieve rather than risk losing any through the colander.

INGREDIENTS

375g (12oz) risoni pasta

7 tbsp extra-virgin olive oil

3 tbsp lemon juice

125g (4oz) feta cheese

2 handfuls of baby spinach

10 radishes

4 tomatoes

2 handfuls of black olives

salt and pepper

2 handfuls of fresh mint

Here's how

Cook the pasta in a large pan of boiling salted water.

Drain the cooked pasta in a sieve and run it under the cold tap.

Tip the pasta back into the pan and dress it with the olive oil and lemon juice.

Dice the feta and roughly chop the spinach. Quarter the radishes and chop the tomatoes. Add the ingredients to the pasta with the olives. Season with salt, pepper and plenty of chopped fresh mint.

Peppers stuffed with risoni & cheese

Pasta comes in all shapes and sizes. Risoni pasta (sometimes called orzo) looks like large grains of rice and it's great for stuffing roasted vegetables. Sunblush tomatoes are halfway between fresh and dried – when you eat one, it still feels like you're eating a fresh plump tangy tomato. Buy them at deli counters preserved in olive oil.

INGREDIENTS

4 red peppers

2 tbsp olive oil

2 tbsp pine nuts

4 handfuls of risoni pasta

200g (7oz) goat's cheese

1 red onion

200g (7oz) sunblush tomatoes

4 tbsp breadcrumbs

extra-virgin olive oil

salt and pepper

Here's how

Pre-heat the oven to 180°C/350°F/Gas Mark 4. Put the whole peppers in an oven tray, drizzle with the olive oil and roast for 25 minutes. Put the pine nuts on a baking tray and toast them in the oven for 4–5 minutes until golden. Don't forget about them – they burn easily.

Cook the pasta in a large pan of boiling salted water. While it is cooking dice the goat's cheese into 2cm (¾in) cubes and place in a bowl. Dice the red onion as finely as possible and add to the goat's cheese. Add the sunblush tomatoes and the toasted pine nuts.

Drain the cooked pasta in a sieve, then run it under the cold tap. Add the pasta to the goat's cheese and vegetables. Season lightly.

Remove the peppers from the oven and leave to cool. Keep the oven on. Cut off the tops of the peppers, pull out the seeds, drain off any juices and sit them back in the oven tray. Fill with the pasta mix and top with the breadcrumbs and a drizzle of olive oil. Return to the oven at the same temperature and bake for 20 minutes until the breadcrumbs are golden.

Pasta with sweet & sour peppers

When I see vibrant red peppers on sale, they say 'buy me, buy me', so I usually end up with far too many in the kitchen. This is a good way to use them up – and you can always preserve a glut of peppers using the recipe on page 14.

INGREDIENTS

375g (12oz) pasta

3 red peppers

1 red onion

1 garlic clove

1 tbsp extra-virgin olive oil

25g (1oz) butter

salt and pepper

5 tbsp balsamic vinegar

75g (3oz) caster sugar

handful of basil, chopped

balsamic dressing (see page 18) to finish

Here's how

Cook the pasta in a large pan of boiling salted water.

While the pasta is cooking, slice the peppers and onion finely and chop the garlic.

Heat a non-stick frying pan on a medium heat. Add the olive oil and butter, followed by the peppers, garlic and onions. Cook until the vegetables are softened – about 5 minutes. Season with a little salt and pepper. Add the vinegar and sugar, and continue to cook until the sugar dissolves.

Drain the cooked pasta in a colander, then stir it into the pan of peppers with the chopped basil. Season with black pepper, add a dash of balsamic dressing to finish the dish, and serve.

Cherry tomatoes with a balsamic dressing

Cherry tomatoes are at their best in the summer, so the least you do to them, the better. Use as many different types as you can find for this dish – red, yellow, orange and purple – and chuck them in with your favourite pasta for a fast supper.

INGREDIENTS

375g (12oz) pasta

1 garlic clove

1 quantity balsamic dressing (see page 18)

400g (13oz) cherry tomatoes, any sort or a mixture

salt and pepper

handful of basil

shaved Parmesan to serve (optional)

Here's how

Cook the pasta in a pan of boiling salted water.

While the pasta is cooking, crush and chop the garlic as finely as possible and add it to the balsamic dressing. Halve the cherry tomatoes and add to the dressing. Season with salt and pepper.

Drain the cooked pasta in a colander. Tip the cherry tomatoes and dressing into the pasta pan, add the pasta and stir together. Finish with lots of fresh basil and a few shavings of Parmesan if you like.

Summer tomato concasse

This is a great way to make a really summery, light and fresh tomato pasta dish. Making a concasse is a Provençal-style way of showcasing the tomatoes, so you must use the very best – don't try making this dish in December!

INGREDIENTS

8 fresh ripe tomatoes

1 garlic clove

375g (12oz) pasta

4 tbsp extra-virgin olive oil

a sprinkle of white sugar

handful of basil

salt and pepper

finely grated Parmesan, to serve

Here's how

Bring a large pan of water to the boil and fill a large bowl with ice-cold water. Cut a small cross at the base of each tomato. When the water is boiling, carefully drop all the tomatoes into the water for 1 minute. Remove them with a slotted spoon and put them straight into the cold water. The tomato skins should now come away easily; remove and discard them. Then cut each tomato in quarters and cut the seeds out with a knife. Throw the seeds away. Dice the tomato flesh and put the diced flesh in a bowl. Chop the garlic finely.

Cook the pasta in the pan of boiling water you used for the tomatoes – I don't like wasting energy or creating more washing up!

Tip the cooked pasta into a colander and stand it in the sink to drain.

Put the pasta pan back on the heat and add the tomato concasse, olive oil and chopped garlic. Warm the tomatoes through, then add just a sprinkle of sugar. Chop the basil and add to the pan with the cooked pasta. Season with salt and pepper, and serve with finely grated Parmesan.

My spaghetti vongole

I first tried this dish in a small town called Montevarchi in Tuscany. My wife and I were waiting for a train to Rome, and the waiter in a scruffy cafe next to the station convinced us to try his mother's cooking. It was the most enjoyable meal I have ever had. Here is my version.

INGREDIENTS

375g (12oz) spaghetti

400g (13oz) can chopped tomatoes

2 tbsp of the best-quality olive oil you can justify, plus more for drizzling

2 garlic cloves

500g (1lb) fresh clams (or more if you are feeling extravagant)

handful of flat-leaf parsley

salt and pepper

Here's how

Cook the spaghetti in a large pan of boiling salted water.

While the pasta is cooking, pour the can of tomatoes into a sieve set over a bowl and let the liquid drain out, leaving just the rich chopped tomatoes.

Meanwhile heat a large non-stick pan and add a couple of tablespoons of olive oil.

Chop the garlic as finely as you can. If you are struggling to chop it, use a fine grater and grate it straight into the frying pan.

Add the clams to the frying pan and cook for 3–4 minutes.

When the spaghetti is cooked, use a pair of tongs to lift it out and drop it straight in with the clams. Do this until you have added all the pasta.

Add the drained tomatoes and the chopped flat-leaf parsley and season with salt and pepper.

Give the whole dish a final drizzle of olive oil and serve.

Black olives with rocket pesto

This dish is one of my quick mid-week suppers. Using my basic tomato pasta sauce (see page 12) allows me to add all sorts of ingredients to bring it to life. If your family is anything like mine, everybody wants something different. So if you make up the basic pasta dish and then put lots of deli pots out on the table, everyone can add whatever they fancy.

INGREDIENTS

375g (12oz) pasta

4 ladlefuls – about 350ml (12fl oz) – basic tomato sauce (see page 12)

16 pitted black olives

4 tbsp rocket pesto (see page 17)

salt and pepper

handful of rocket leaves, chopped, to garnish

2–3 tbsp extra-virgin olive oil

grated Parmesan cheese, to finish (optional)

Here's how

Cook the pasta in a large pan of boiling salted water.

Tip the cooked pasta into a colander and stand it in the sink to drain.

Put the tomato sauce, olives and pesto into the pasta pan and warm through on a low heat. Add the pasta and stir together until all the pasta is coated.

Serve up the pasta with a little black pepper, a scattering of chopped rocket leaves, a drizzle of extra-virgin olive oil and some Parmesan if you like.

Autumn

Autumn creeps up on us almost without notice. Before we know it, there's a nip in the air first thing and it's dark when we leave work for the day. But it's not all doom and gloom: autumn brings a world of gastronomic goodies to enjoy.

Ham hock & peas

This recipe uses a slow cooker. Stick it on in the morning and dinner's nearly ready when you get in from work. By the way, don't throw away the cooking liquid. Leave it in the slow cooker, add half a bag of frozen peas and turn it on to full power for 1 hour. Blend the resulting soup with 100ml (3½fl oz) of crème fraîche and you've got tomorrow's lunch – or freeze it for later.

INGREDIENTS

1 onion

1 carrot

1 celery stick

1 ham hock, weighing about 750g (1½lb)

375g (12oz) pasta

250g (8oz) frozen peas

handful of flat-leaf parsley, chopped

2 tbsp extra-virgin olive oil

salt and pepper

75g (3oz) Parmesan, grated, to serve

Here's how

Roughly chop the onion, carrot and celery and place in a slow cooker with the ham hock.

Top up the cooker with water and set it to cook for 8 hours on medium during the day.

When you get home, turn off the cooker and remove the ham. Place it in a bowl to cool.

Cook the pasta and peas together in a large pan of boiling salted water. Shred the meat from the ham bone and roughly chop if necessary. Drain the cooked pasta and peas in a colander. Tip them back into the empty pan. Add the meat, followed by the chopped parsley, olive oil and 2 tbsp of the cooking juices from the slow cooker. Give the pan a good stir to make sure the pasta gets coated. Season with black pepper and serve with grated Parmesan.

Walnut pesto

I first came across this dish in Arezzo, a small town in Tuscany. Pesto is popular these days and I urge you to try this version. The walnuts give it a wonderful powerfully nutty flavour that works well with Parmesan.

INGREDIENTS

375g (12oz) pasta

100g (3½oz) toasted walnuts (see page 16), plus a handful to serve

3 garlic cloves, peeled

50g (2oz) Parmesan, grated, plus extra to serve

1 tsp salt

pepper

sprig of rosemary, leaves stripped

slice of bread, white or brown

7 tbsp extra-virgin olive oil

zest and juice of ½ lemon

sage leaves, to serve

Here's how

Pre-heat the oven to 180°C/350°F/Gas Mark 4.

Cook the pasta in a large pan of boiling salted water.

While the pasta is cooking, make the pesto. Put the toasted walnuts in a food processor with the garlic, grated cheese, salt, pepper, rosemary and bread. Blend the ingredients, then pour in the olive oil while the blender is running, until you get a smooth paste.

Taste the pesto before adding the lemon zest and a little juice to help balance the richness.

Drain the cooked pasta in a colander. As you drain it, whip the pan under the colander to catch the last few drips of the cooking water – the starch from the pasta helps make your sauce creamier.

Put a few spoonfuls of the pesto into the pasta pan with the cooking water; add the drained pasta and give it a big stir to make sure the pasta is coated.

Serve with a few extra toasted walnuts, sage leaves, some grated Parmesan and a few twists of black pepper.

Roasted squash with ricotta & sage

Roasting the butternut squash intensifies its delicious flavour, so it's worth that bit of extra time in the kitchen. And sage is the perfect accompaniment to its sweet roasted flesh. Combining the two of them with the creaminess of ricotta makes for a great dish.

INGREDIENTS

1 butternut squash – you need about 1kg (2lb) prepared flesh

salt and pepper

sprig of rosemary

2 tbsp olive oil

375g (12oz) spaghetti

250g (8oz) homemade ricotta (see page 20)

extra-virgin olive oil, to drizzle (optional)

4 sage leaves

50g (2oz) Parmesan or Pecorino, grated

Here's how

Pre-heat the oven to 180°C/350°F/Gas Mark 4.

Cut the squash down the middle and scoop out the seeds with a spoon. Using a sharp knife score the flesh. Put the squash on a baking tray and season with salt and pepper, scatter with rosemary leaves and drizzle with olive oil. Roast in the oven until soft – about 45 minutes.

Meanwhile cook the pasta in a large pan of boiling salted water. Tip the cooked pasta into a colander and stand it in the sink to drain.

When the squash is cooked, leave to cool, then scoop out the flesh and chop into small pieces. Put the squash and the ricotta in a pan, and add a drizzle of extr-virgin olive oil if you like. Then add the cooked pasta and mix together over a low heat to warm through.

Shred the sage leaves and scatter over the pasta with the grated cheese.

Mushrooms & rosemary

Mushrooms and rosemary go so well together it makes perfect sense for me to put them together in a great bowl of pasta. Whenever you fry mushrooms, they start to seep out water, so you need to carry on cooking them until the water evaporates, to intensify their flavour.

INGREDIENTS

375g (12oz) pasta

500g (1lb) brown chestnut mushrooms

2 garlic cloves

1 tbsp rosemary leaves

2–3 tbsp olive oil

squeeze of lemon juice

200g (7oz) tub crème fraîche

salt and pepper

Here's how

Cook the pasta in a large pan of boiling salted water.

While the pasta is cooking, slice the mushrooms and chop the garlic and rosemary. Place a frying pan on a low heat to warm. Pour 2–3 tbsp olive oil into the pan. Add the mushrooms, garlic and rosemary.

Resist stirring the ingredients around too much. Let the water evaporate from the mushrooms: you want them to be golden and caramelised – that's the process that generates the flavour. This should take about 5 minutes. Add a squeeze of lemon juice and the crème fraîche.

Drain the cooked pasta and mix in with the mushrooms. Season with a little salt and pepper and serve.

Crayfish linguine

Crayfish have a real meaty texture to them and make a great addition to pasta. Pick up a tub from your local deli or supermarket deli counter for a quick mid-week supper. Draining the tomatoes – canned or fresh – prevents the sauce being too watery.

INGREDIENTS

375g (12oz) pasta

200g (7oz) canned chopped tomatoes or 3 fresh tomatoes

2 tbsp extra-virgin olive oil

juice of ½ lemon

225g (7½oz) deli tub of cooked crayfish tails

1 tbsp chopped flat-leaf parsley

salt and pepper

Here's how

Cook the pasta in a large pan of boiling salted water.

Put the canned tomatoes into a sieve to drain or chop the fresh tomatoes, deseed and leave them to drain in a sieve.

Tip the cooked pasta into a colander and stand it in the sink to drain.

Pour the olive oil and lemon juice into the pasta pan and whisk to make a dressing. Add the crayfish tails, followed by the diced tomatoes and chopped flat-leaf parsley and warm over a medium heat.

Stir in the pasta and add plenty of black pepper.

Fennel & tomato ragu

I am a big fan of fennel and tomato. Why not try going veggie tonight with this easy ragu?
A ragu is a northern Italian-style tomato sauce, and by using my basic tomato sauce straight
from your fridge, you can have supper on the table in less than 15 minutes.

INGREDIENTS

375g (12oz) pasta

2 fennel bulbs

1 garlic clove

2 tbsp olive oil

½ glass of dry white wine

**3 ladlefuls – about 250ml (8fl oz)
– basic tomato sauce
(see page 12)**

salt and pepper

Here's how

Cook the pasta in a large pan of boiling salted water.

While the pasta is cooking, prepare the fennel. Cut the top and bottom
off the bulb, reserving a few fronds to serve with the finished dish. Cut the
bulb down the middle to expose the core. Using a smaller knife, cut out and
throw away the solid white middle bit as it won't soften during cooking.
Dice the rest of the fennel into small chunks. Chop the garlic. Place a
medium pan on the heat to warm. Add the fennel, garlic and olive oil.

Using a wooden spoon, keep stirring the fennel so it does not stick. After
5 minutes or so, add the wine. After a further 5 minutes the wine will have
reduced by half. At this point add the tomato sauce and simmer until the
fennel is tender – the best way to check is to taste it.

Drain the cooked pasta and add it to the sauce. Stir to mix, then serve
scattered with fronds of fennel.

Blue cheese & toasted walnuts

Blue cheese and toasted walnuts are made for each other. Here's how to turn them into a great quick supper. Toasting the walnuts then seasoning them with honey makes all the difference. You can't used ready-roasted walnuts for this recipe as they need to be warm to absorb the honey.

INGREDIENTS

375g (12oz) pasta

handful of walnuts

100g (3½oz) blue cheese of your choice

1 tsp honey

sea salt

3 sage leaves, finely chopped

salt and pepper

2 tbsp extra-virgin olive oil

Here's how

Pre-heat the oven to 180°C/350°F/Gas Mark 4.

Cook the pasta in a large pan of boiling salted water.

While the pasta is cooking, put the walnuts on a baking tray and toast them in the oven for 7 minutes – watch them as they can burn really quickly.

Dice the blue cheese into 1cm (½in) cubes.

When the walnuts are ready, take them out of the oven and season with the honey and a sprinkle of sea salt. It's important to do this while they are still warm, as the honey will coat the nuts easily.

Tip the cooked pasta into a colander and stand it in the sink to drain. Add the cheese, walnuts and chopped sage to the pasta pan. Put the pasta back in the pan, give everything a quick stir and season with black pepper and add the extra-virgin olive oil. Taste before you add any extra salt – blue cheese can be salty.

Mushrooms with Taleggio

Taleggio cheese has an amazing richness to it. As it melts over the pasta it almost creates a sauce for you – match that with some fab mushrooms cooked with a little garlic and rosemary and you've got a winner.

INGREDIENTS

375g (12oz) tagliatelle

300g (10oz) mushrooms

2 tbsp olive oil

sea salt

1 garlic clove

sprig of rosemary, leaves chopped

handful of flat-leaf parsley, chopped

50g (2oz) butter

150g (5oz) Taleggio cheese

black pepper

extra-virgin olive oil to serve

Here's how

Cook the tagliatelle in a large pan of boiling salted water.

While the pasta is cooking, cut the mushrooms in half. Place a non-stick frying pan on a medium heat to warm. Add the mushrooms to the hot pan, cut side down, with the olive oil and a sprinkle of sea salt – the salt draws the moisture out and helps the mushrooms take on lots of flavour. Don't stir the mushrooms. Crush the garlic and add to the pan with the chopped rosemary, parsley and butter. This is when the magic starts to happen: as these flavours marry in the pan, I guarantee your mouth will water.

Turn the mushrooms over after about 5 minutes or when they are a rich golden colour.

Lift out the cooked pasta using a pair of tongs and place it in the pan with the mushrooms.

Cut the cheese into chunks and add them to the pan. Give it a little stir around – as the cheese hits the hot pasta it will start to melt and create a rich sauce. Serve straight away with a little black pepper and a touch of good-quality extra-virgin olive oil.

Mushroom pesto

I love pesto – it's one of my favourite things to mix into some pasta. When I was in Tuscany I came across this idea. It's a great dish to introduce people to mushrooms. I've met so many people who say they don't like mushrooms – but they love this.

INGREDIENTS

375g (12oz) pasta

For the mushroom pesto

500g (1lb) mushrooms

100ml (3½fl oz) extra-virgin olive oil

sea salt

100g (3½oz) walnuts

75g (3oz) Parmesan, plus extra to serve

sprig of rosemary, leaves only

½ slice of bread

2 garlic cloves, peeled

squeeze of lemon juice

pepper

Here's how

Cook the pasta in a large pan of boiling salted water.

While the pasta is cooking, slice the mushrooms. Place a non-stick frying pan over a medium heat to warm. Put the mushrooms in the frying pan with a drizzle of the olive oil and a sprinkle of sea salt.

Cook the mushrooms for 5–6 minutes to intensify their flavour. They should take on a nice golden colour.

When the mushrooms are cooked, transfer most of them to a food processor, reserving a few slices to serve. Add the walnuts, Parmesan, rosemary, bread and garlic. Blend until smooth, then add the remaining olive oil and a squeeze of lemon juice. Season with salt and pepper.

Drain the cooked pasta in a colander. Spoon the pesto into the warm pasta pan. Add the cooked pasta and stir to mix. Serve with grated Parmesan and the reserved mushroom slices.

Pasta melanzane

Melanzane is a great combination of grilled aubergine, mozzarella and a tomato sauce, usually baked in the oven. I've used those same ingredients to create a pasta sauce, but I've still roasted the vegetables in the oven in the classic way to get the same effect.

INGREDIENTS

salt and pepper

2 tbsp extra-virgin olive oil

2 medium aubergines

375g (12oz) pasta spirals or fusilli

125g (4oz) fresh mozzarella ball

punnet of cherry tomatoes, halved

1 ladleful – about 100ml (3½fl oz) – basic tomato sauce (see page 12)

handful of fresh basil, leaves torn

Here's how

Pre-heat the oven to 180°C/350°F/Gas Mark 4.

Season a baking tray with salt, pepper and extra-virgin olive oil. Slice the aubergines lengthways into ½cm (¼in) slices and lay them on the tray. Turn the slices over so that both sides are seasoned. Bake for 20 minutes.

After about 10 minutes start cooking the pasta in a large pan of boiling salted water.

Remove the aubergine slices from the oven, cut them in half and place them in a bowl. Tear up the mozzarella and add to the bowl, followed by the cherry tomatoes.

Tip the cooked pasta into a colander and stand it in the sink to drain. Add the tomato sauce, aubergines, mozzarella, torn basil and the cherry tomatoes to the pasta pan to warm.

Add the drained pasta, mix together and serve.

Tomato soup with olives

I love having a great tasty soup for my lunch or even for dinner with some nice crusty bread – sometimes it's just as satisfying as a square meal. If you make plenty you can always take a flask to work with you.

INGREDIENTS

1 onion

1 carrot

2 celery sticks

2 tbsp olive oil

2 garlic cloves

sprig of rosemary

3 sage leaves

2 x 400g (13oz) cans chopped
   tomatoes

600ml (1 pint) vegetable stock

2 tbsp tomato purée

100g (3½oz) black olives

150g (5oz) pasta for soup: hoops
   (anelli) or tubes (ditalini)

salt and pepper

handful of basil leaves, chopped

3 tbsp extra-virgin olive oil

Here's how

Using a sharp knife, dice the vegetables into small pieces: the smaller you cut them, the quicker they will cook.

Place a large saucepan on a low heat to warm. Add the olive oil followed by the vegetables. Cook on a medium heat for 5 minutes or so until they start to soften.

Chop the garlic, rosemary and sage and add to the pan. Add the canned tomatoes and the vegetable stock and tomato purée. Turn the heat up.

After 10 minutes add the olives and the pasta, and give the soup a good stir so the pasta doesn't stick together. Taste the pasta after about 9 minutes to check that it's cooked. Season with salt and pepper. Finally to make the soup taste really amazing, add the chopped basil and extra-virgin olive oil.

Pumpkin & roasted garlic lasagne

Pumpkins are one of the few truly seasonal ingredients. I find it refreshing that there are some things you just can't buy all year round – nature's won that battle. This was one of the first dishes I puréed for my daughter Poppy. Now she's three and a half and won't eat it! Kids...

INGREDIENTS

1 medium pumpkin – you need about 1kg (2lb) prepared flesh

salt and pepper

2 tbsp olive oil, plus extra for drizzling

1 bulb of garlic

2 ladlefuls – about 175ml (6fl oz) – basic tomato sauce (see page 12)

8 fresh lasagne sheets

100g (3½oz) Parmesan, grated

400g (13oz) tub full-fat crème fraîche

125g (4oz) mozzarella ball

Here's how

Pre-heat the oven to 180°C/350°F/Gas Mark 4.

Using a large sharp knife, cut the pumpkin into 8 portions. Scoop out the seeds with a spoon. Put the pumpkin portions on a baking tray and season with lots of salt and pepper, and add a good drizzle of olive oil. Cut the garlic in half and place on the baking tray with the pumpkin. Roast them in the oven for 45 minutes to help intensify the sweet pumpkin flavour.

The roast pumpkin will be soft and caramelised and the garlic will be soft. Leave them until cool enough to handle. Cut the pumpkin into chunks and place in a bowl. Squeeze the roast garlic into the bowl and stir to mix.

Place half the mixture in the base of an ovenproof dish. Add a ladleful of tomato sauce and top with a layer of fresh lasagne. Repeat the process, finishing with a layer of lasagne.

Stir the Parmesan into the crème fraîche and add a few twists of black pepper. Spoon the mixture on top of the lasagne. Tear up the mozzarella and scatter on top. Drizzle with olive oil then put it in the oven at the same temperature. Cook for 40 minutes until golden and bubbling.

Slow-cooked beef in red wine

It's that time of year when you need to bring out the slow cooker again – it's a great way to create a fantastic flavoursome dish. Using a whole bulb of garlic gives the dish a wonderful rich, sweet flavour and an amazing amount of depth.

INGREDIENTS

4 tbsp flour

salt and pepper

1kg (2lb) diced beef

2 tbsp olive oil

1 large onion

2 carrots

1 bulb of garlic

½ red chilli (optional)

sprig of rosemary

250ml (8fl oz) red wine

600ml (1 pint) beef stock

100g (3½oz) black olives

50g (2oz) risoni pasta

Here's how

Put the flour in a bowl and season with plenty of salt and pepper. Roll the diced beef in the flour and shake off any excess. Place a non-stick frying pan on a low heat. Pour the olive oil into the frying pan.

Fry the beef to seal in all the flavours and get a great colour into your dish. Do this in a few batches. If you overfill the pan you won't get a good sizzle – and sizzle means lots of flavour.

Put the beef in the slow cooker. Dice the vegetables and add to the cooker. Cut the garlic bulb across and just put it in as it is. Chop the chilli and rosemary and add to the cooker. Finally add the red wine and beef stock.

Set the slow cooker to cook for 8 hours. Or make this dish in the oven: cook it at 150°C/300°F/Gas Mark 2 for 3 hours. About 30 minutes before end of cooking time, add the olives and the pasta, give the dish a stir and finish cooking. Before you serve the dish, you need to fish around to find the garlic bulb, lift it out and carefully squeeze out the flesh into the red wine stock. Just make sure you don't burn your hands: if necessary, leave the garlic to cool and then do it.

Roasted marrow with Pecorino

No one ever seems to know what to do with marrows. People always ask me how to make them taste exciting. Here's my favourite way of serving marrow, shown to me by an Italian lad who spent the summer working with me to improve his English – his cooking wasn't bad either!

INGREDIENTS

1 marrow

1 bulb of garlic

6–7 tbsp extra-virgin olive oil

salt and pepper

squeeze of lemon juice

375g (12oz) pappardelle pasta

75g (3oz) Pecorino, grated

1 tsp chopped sage

1 tsp chopped rosemary

torn basil to serve

Here's how

Heat the oven to 180°C/350°F/Gas Mark 4.

Cut the marrow into large chunks and place on a roasting tray. Smash the bulb of garlic, peel the cloves and put them on the tray with the marrow. Drizzle with 2 tbsp olive oil and season with plenty of salt and pepper. Roast for 45 minutes until soft and golden. Leave to cool, then scoop the marrow flesh away from the skin.

Put the marrow into the food processor with the garlic cloves. Add a squeeze of lemon juice and the remaining olive oil and blend. Season with salt and pepper to taste.

Cook the pappardelle in a large pan of boiling salted water. Drain the cooked pasta in a colander and return to the pan. Add the marrow and stir together thoroughly.

Finish with grated Pecorino and chopped herbs.

The last of the tomatoes pasta bake

Ok, it's time you used up the very last of those tomatoes you've been nurturing all summer on the patio. This dish will help you appreciate all the hard work you've put into growing them – you really can't beat the taste of home-grown tomatoes.

INGREDIENTS

375g (12oz) large pasta shells such as conchiglioni

8 tomatoes

8 tsp homemade ricotta (see page 20)

extra-virgin olive oil

handful of basil, leaves chopped

50g (2oz) Parmesan, grated

6 tbsp breadcrumbs

salt and pepper

Here's how

Pre-heat the oven to 180°C/350°F/Gas Mark 4.

Cook the pasta shells in a large pan of boiling salted water.

While the pasta is cooking, cut the tomatoes into quarters. If you have time, scoop out the tomato seeds.

Drain the cooked shells in a colander, then transfer them straight to an ovenproof dish. Scatter the chopped tomatoes on top. Using a teaspoon, place little nuggets of ricotta cheese into the pasta shells.

Drizzle over some extra-virgin olive oil followed by plenty of chopped basil.

Mix the Parmesan and breadcrumbs together in a bowl, then scatter over the pasta.

Season with a little salt and pepper and maybe an extra little splash of extra-virgin olive oil and bake for 25 minutes until the top just starts to crisp up.

Autumn broth

This soup has a great, deep, dark and earthy flavour that really shows off the mushrooms to their best. Sometimes only dried mushrooms will do in a particular recipe – you just don't get the same intense flavour from fresh.

INGREDIENTS

1 onion

3 garlic cloves

2 tbsp olive oil

handful of dried mushrooms

600ml (1 pint) vegetable stock

1 red pepper

bunch of spring onions

375g (12oz) readymade gnocchi

salt and pepper

Here's how

Chop the onion and garlic as finely as you can. Place a medium pan on a low heat. Add the onion and garlic with the olive oil and cook until soft.

Add the dried mushrooms and stock and simmer for 15 minutes until the mushrooms are nice and soft.

Meanwhile cut the red pepper into strips and chop the spring onions roughly. Add the pepper to the pan when the mushrooms have softened, followed by the gnocchi.

When the gnocchi start to rise to the top of the pan, turn off the heat. Add the chopped spring onions, season and serve.

Venison ragu

Frosty autumn mornings mean game season to me. There's nothing better than great British game – it's full of flavour, free range and plentiful. Here's my recipe for a hearty venison ragu – one of those dishes it's great to come back to after a ramble over the hills.

INGREDIENTS

1 medium onion

1 carrot

1 celery stick

2 tbsp olive oil

4 rashers of pancetta or smoked streaky bacon

350g (11½oz) diced venison

2 tbsp tomato purée

1 tsp sugar

150ml (¼ pint) red wine

1 tbsp chopped rosemary

2 juniper berries

salt and pepper

500ml (17fl oz) beef stock

100ml (3½fl oz) full-fat milk

375g (12oz) penne pasta

handful of flat-leaf parsley

grated Parmesan, to serve

Here's how

Finely chop the vegetables. Heat the olive oil in a saucepan, add the pancetta or bacon and cook over a medium heat for 2–3 minutes until just browning. Add the onion, carrot and celery, and cook for 5 minutes until beginning to brown.

Add the venison and cook, stirring it around until golden brown.

Stir in the tomato purée, sugar and red wine. Add the chopped rosemary and juniper berries. Bring to the boil and allow the liquid to reduce until it has nearly disappeared.

Season with salt and pepper, then add half the stock. Bring to the boil, then turn the heat down to a simmer and cook for about 1½ hours. Check the pan from time to time and top up with more stock if the mixture looks too thick and sticky. Stir in the milk, then simmer for a further 15 minutes until thick and creamy.

Meanwhile cook the pasta in a large pan of boiling salted water. Serve with the ragu, sprinkled with parsley and Parmesan.

Chorizo, tomato & olives

Chorizo sausage adds a real punch of flavour to a dish with a minimum effort. That's my idea of how to make cooking easy. This is one of the simplest recipes in my book, yet it loses nothing in the way of flavour or good looks!

INGREDIENTS

375g (12oz) penne pasta
200g (7oz) chorizo sausage
8 fresh plum tomatoes
handful of pitted black olives
salt and pepper

Here's how

Cook the pasta in a large pan of boiling salted water.

While the pasta is cooking, slice the chorizo sausage. Cut the tomatoes into quarters.

Heat a non-stick frying pan and add the chorizo and tomatoes. As the pan heats up it will melt the natural fats in the chorizo sausage, so you don't need to add any oil.

Drain the cooked pasta and add it to the frying pan with the olives. Season with salt and pepper.

Meatballs with juniper & tomato

We Brits are great at making all kinds of different sausages. To me, you can tell a good butcher by his sausages. I've used wild boar ones to make this heart-warming pasta dish but really any great British banger will do – just use your favourite.

INGREDIENTS

375g (12oz) pasta

4 ladlefuls – about 350ml (12fl oz) – basic tomato sauce (see page 12)

2 juniper berries

1 tbsp chopped rosemary

8 wild boar sausages

Here's how

Cook the pasta in a large pan of boiling salted water.

While the pasta is cooking, put the tomato sauce in another pan over a medium heat.

Using the back of a knife, squash the juniper berries to release the flavour. Add them to the tomato sauce with the rosemary.

Cut the sausage skin away with a pair of scissors. Discard the skin. Wet your hands under the tap and roll the sausages into small meatballs (the water on your hands stops the sausagemeat from sticking). Drop the meatballs into the simmering sauce and cook for 10 minutes.

Drain the cooked pasta, add to the sauce and you're done.

Winter

Dark winter mornings and evenings really get me, so I like to breathe a bit of life and energy into my winter cooking, while still aiming for that comforting, warm feeling that we all crave at this time of year. So when it's dark outside make sure your kitchen is buzzing with these great dishes – they don't take forever to cook but they will warm you up.

Sweet onions & thyme

The key to this dish is cooking the onions long and slow to extract the sweetness. To save time you could even cook the onions the night before and keep them in the fridge. Then when you get in from work, all you've got to do is to warm them up gently and cook the pasta.

INGREDIENTS

2 medium onions

1 garlic clove

2 tbsp olive oil

1 tbsp sea salt

375g (12oz) pasta

2 tbsp chopped thyme

1 tsp balsamic vinegar

75g (3oz) Pecorino, grated

extra-virgin olive oil, to serve

Here's how

Peel and slice the onions as finely as possible. Chop the garlic. Place a frying pan on a low heat. Pour in the olive oil followed by the onions and garlic. Add the sea salt to draw out the moisture and help the onions caramelise. Let the onions cook for at least 20 minutes until they take on a sweet golden-brown colour.

After 10 minutes put a large pan of salted water on to boil. Cook the pasta in the boiling water. Add the chopped thyme and balsamic vinegar to the onions.

Drain the cooked pasta and stir it into the onions.

Serve with grated Pecorino and a drizzle of extra-virgin olive oil.

Parsnip, Parmesan & chilli

Here's a quick tasty way to warm up when you come in from a day's gardening or a long walk. The sweetness of the parsnips works really well with a hint of chilli. And this is one recipe where adding a little of the pasta's cooking water can help create a creamy sauce.

INGREDIENTS

375g (12oz) pasta
2 garlic cloves
sprig of rosemary
1 red chilli
2 tbsp olive oil
6 parsnips
100g (3½oz) Parmesan
salt and pepper

Here's how

Cook the pasta in a large pan of boiling salted water.

While the pasta is cooking, peel and chop the garlic, and chop the rosemary leaves. Deseed and dice the chilli.

Place a large frying pan on the heat. Add the garlic, rosemary and olive oil. While they start to gently sizzle, peel and grate the parsnips and add to the pan. Cook for 7–8 minutes so the parsnips soften.

Drain the cooked pasta in a colander, keeping back a little cooking water by putting the pan back under the colander to catch the last few drips.

Add the pasta to the parsnips in the frying pan. Stir to mix thoroughly.

Grate the Parmesan straight into the pan using a microplane or fine grater. If the pasta looks a bit dry, add a little of the cooking water. Add the diced chilli, season with black pepper and serve.

For a variation on this dish, try adding 250g (8oz) pancetta when you fry the garlic.

Smoked haddock carbonara

Carbonara is probably one of the first pasta dishes I learnt to cook, so I've been making it for a while! This recipe is similar to the traditional dish but it uses smoked haddock instead of bacon, to create a lighter-tasting carbonara.

INGREDIENTS

2 fillets of naturally smoked haddock, about 150g (5oz) each

300ml (½ pint) milk

375g (12oz) spaghetti

150ml (¼ pint) crème fraîche

salt and pepper

handful of fresh chives, chopped

squeeze of lemon juice

grated Parmesan, to serve

Here's how

Preheat the oven to 180°C/350°F/Gas Mark 4. Place the haddock in an ovenproof dish and pour over the milk. Cover with foil and bake in the oven for 15–20 minutes until the fish is cooked.

Meanwhile cook the spaghetti in a large pan of boiling salted water.

When the fish is cooked, heat a large non-stick frying pan. Carefully pour into the frying pan the milk that the fish was cooked in, and simmer until reduced by half.

Add the crème fraîche and turn the heat right down.

Drain the cooked pasta and add to the pan.

Carefully break up the haddock and add to the pasta. Heat through and finally season with a little black pepper, chopped chives and a squeeze of lemon juice. Serve with grated Parmesan.

Leek, ham & crème fraîche bake

This is a great winter warmer. Leeks and ham work really well together, and the ham just cuts the richness of the cream and leeks, adding a contrasting saltiness. The ham really takes the place of lasagne and gives the dish a bit of a boost.

INGREDIENTS

4 medium leeks

100ml (3½fl oz) dry white wine

50g (2oz) butter

salt and pepper

375g (12oz) pasta

6 tbsp crème fraîche

150g (5oz) Parmesan, grated

6 slices ham

2–3 tbsp breadcrumbs

2–3 tbsp olive oil

Here's how

Pre-heat the oven to 180°C/350°F/Gas Mark 4.

Slice the leeks into 2cm (¾in) round slices and put them in the bottom of an ovenproof dish. Add the white wine, butter and season generously with salt and pepper. Cover with foil and bake in the oven for 25 minutes until the leeks are nice and tender.

While the leeks are in the oven cook the pasta in a large pan of boiling salted water.

Drain the cooked pasta and return it to the pan. Spoon in the crème fraîche, add 75g (3oz) of the Parmesan and season.

Remove the leeks from the oven and leave to cool for a moment, then carefully drain away the excess liquid. Leave the oven on.

Lay the slices of ham over the leeks – just as if they were sheets of lasagne. Pile the creamy pasta on top of the ham and leeks.

Mix the breadcrumbs and the remaining Parmesan with the olive oil. Scatter the breadcrumb mixture over the top and bake for 20 minutes until golden and crispy. The dish doesn't really need cooking – it's just to give it a nice crunch on top.

Sun-dried tomatoes & cream cheese

This is probably my quickest and easiest supper dish, but it's still packed full of flavour and very satisfying. You can add any extras you have in the fridge – preserved roasted peppers (see page 14), maybe a little salami or even some canned sweetcorn.

INGREDIENTS

375g (12oz) pasta

4 tbsp homemade basil pesto (see page 17)

4 tbsp cream cheese

2 tbsp milk

4 sun-dried tomatoes, chopped

75g (3oz) toasted pine nuts (see page 16)

handful of basil, leaves chopped or torn

Here's how

Cook the pasta in a large pan of boiling salted water. Tip the cooked pasta into a colander and leave it in the sink to drain.

Put the pesto, cream cheese and milk in the pasta pan. Using a wooden spoon, mix them together to create a rich creamy sauce. Add the cooked pasta, sun-dried tomatoes, toasted pine nuts and basil and it's ready to eat.

Sausage meatballs with spaghetti

Sausages are an ideal starting point for a quick substantial dinner. The butcher has done most of the work – I've just added some garlic, chilli and fennel to remind me of the amazing flavour of *finocchiona*, my favourite salami from Tuscany.

INGREDIENTS

2 onions

4 x 400g (13oz) cans of tomatoes

1 bulb of garlic, cloves peeled, plus 2 extra cloves

2 vegetable stock cubes

handful of basil, plus extra to serve (or a few tsp pesto)

1 tsp fennel seeds

1 red chilli

6 Cumberland sausages

375g (12oz) spaghetti

Here's how

Chop the onions into quarters and place in a large saucepan with the tins of chopped tomatoes, the cloves from the garlic bulb (keep back the 2 extra cloves) and stock cubes and simmer for 40 minutes until the onions are soft. Leave to cool for 30 minutes, then add a handful of basil or a few tsp of pesto. Use a stick blender to whizz up the sauce until smooth.

Using a pestle and mortar, bash the fennel seeds to release the flavour. Peel and crush the remaining garlic cloves. Deseed and chop the chilli. Put the garlic and chilli in a bowl with the fennel seeds. Using a pair of scissors, cut the sausages out of their skins and add to the bowl. (Discard the skins.)

Mix the sausagemeat and flavourings together. Wet your hands under the tap and roll the mixture into small meatballs (the water on your hands stops the sausagemeat from sticking).

Place the meatballs in the pasta sauce and simmer for 10–15 minutes until the meatballs are cooked. Meanwhile, cook the spaghetti in a large pan of boiling salted water. Drain the pasta, stir into the sauce and serve with a few extra basil leaves if using.

Pasta al forno

The great thing about pasta bakes is that you can add any little extras that take your fancy – any leftovers from lunch or bits and pieces hanging around in the fridge – the tomato sauce links them all together. Al forno simply means from the oven in Italian.

INGREDIENTS

375g (12oz) pasta

4 ladlefuls – about 350ml (12fl oz) – of basic tomato sauce (see page 12)

extras or leftovers, such as olives, sunblush tomatoes, tuna, cooked chicken, roasted vegetables

handful of basil, leaves chopped

salt and pepper

125g (4oz) hard cow's milk mozzarella, grated

Optional topping

1 garlic clove

2–3 tbsp breadcrumbs

2 tbsp olive oil

Here's how

Pre-heat the oven to 180˚C/350˚F/Gas Mark 4.

Cook the pasta in a large pan of boiling salted water. Drain the cooked pasta in a colander, then tip the pasta back into the pan. Add the tomato sauce and any other little extras that take your fancy from the fridge or cupboard. Add the chopped basil. Season and stir to mix.

Pour the pasta and sauce into an ovenproof dish.

Sprinkle the grated mozzarella over the top of the pasta.

For the optional topping, chop the garlic finely and add to the breadcrumbs in a small bowl. Pour the olive oil over the crumbs and mix so the oil soaks in. Scatter the breadcrumbs over the top of the pasta bake.

Cook in the oven for 15 minutes until the cheese has melted and the breadcrumb topping is crunchy.

Fennel & leeks with leftover chicken

We always end up with leftovers when we roast a chicken on a Sunday. As a kid I have fond memories of my dad in the kitchen picking the meat off the chicken while the dog sat there licking its lips in anticipation. I found myself in the very same situation the other day. I guess it's inevitable – we all turn into our parents in some way or another. If, like me, you have roasted your chicken with fennel, you can use some leftover cooked fennel; if not, follow the first steps of the recipe.

INGREDIENTS

1 bulb of fennel

2 leeks, washed and trimmed

sea salt

100ml (3½fl oz) white wine

375g (12oz) pasta

6 tbsp double cream

300g (10oz) cooked chicken torn into small bite-size pieces

1 tbsp chopped fresh tarragon

salt and pepper

Here's how

Cut the top and bottom off the fennel, then cut it down the middle and remove the white core. Dice the rest of the fennel into small pieces – the smaller they are, the quicker they cook. Slice the leeks finely. Place the leeks and fennel in a saucepan on a medium heat. Sprinkle with a little sea salt, followed by the white wine. Turn the heat up and cook until tender.

Meanwhile cook the pasta in a large pan of boiling salted water.

When the fennel and leeks are cooked, stir in the cream, then add the cooked chicken and chopped tarragon. Have a quick taste and check the seasoning. Then add the cooked, drained pasta and give it all a good stir.

Macaroni cheese & chorizo

A rich feel-good dish – the hidden nuggets of smoky chorizo sausage take you by surprise. Chorizo may not be a typical Italian ingredient but it is one of my favourite store-cupboard standbys as it adds such a kick of flavour to almost any dish.

INGREDIENTS

375g (12oz) macaroni pasta

50g (2oz) butter

50g (2oz) flour

600ml (1 pint) milk

100g (3½oz) strong Cheddar, grated

150g (5oz) chorizo sausage, diced

Here's how

Pre-heat the oven to 180°C/350°F/Gas Mark 4.

Cook the pasta in plenty of boiling salted water.

While the pasta is cooking, make the sauce. Melt the butter in a medium saucepan, add the flour and mix well. Keep stirring for a minute to cook the flour. Add the milk a little at a time and keep mixing. Turn the heat down and continue to add the milk gradually until you have a smooth sauce.

Take the pan off the heat and add half the cheese. Mix in until it has melted. Stir in the diced chorizo sausage.

Drain the cooked pasta and mix into the sauce. Pour into an ovenproof dish, top with the remaining cheese and bake in the oven until the top is golden – about 25 minutes – and your mouth is watering.

Avocado, mint, chilli & feta salad

This fresh-tasting salad is just the kind of lift you need to tickle your taste buds in winter. Remember to wash your hands after chopping the chilli – you'll soon know about it if you don't and then absent-mindedly rub your eyes!

INGREDIENTS

375g (12oz) farfalle pasta

zest and juice of 2 limes

7 tbsp extra-virgin olive oil

1 ripe avocado

1 red chilli

handful of fresh mint

1 red onion

salt and pepper

200g (7oz) feta cheese

Here's how

Cook the pasta in a large pan of boiling salted water.

While the pasta is cooking, prepare the limes. If they are rock hard, pop them in the microwave for 10 seconds to soften, then roll them on a chopping board before grating the zest and squeezing the juice. Mix the zest, juice and olive oil to make a dressing.

Cut the avocado down the middle, cutting around the stone. Pop the stone out of the centre and skin the avocado. Cut the flesh into chunks and place in a bowl with the salad dressing, to stop it going brown.

Deseed and chop the chilli. Chop the mint leaves. Add them both to the dressing. Chop the onion.

Drain the cooked pasta in a colander and refresh under the cold tap. Drain the pasta well. Transfer it to the bowl with the dressing, avocado and chopped onion.

Mix the salad together ensuring all the pasta is coated by the dressing. Season, crumble the feta over the top and serve.

Baked gnocchi

I love gnocchi and I really enjoy making them – but that's more of a weekend job. Readymade gnocchi are easily available: all you need to do is put them together with some tasty sauce, top with cheese and pop the dish in the oven for a fab gnocchi bake.

INGREDIENTS

375g (12oz) packet of fresh gnocchi

4 ladlefuls – about 350ml (12fl oz) – of basic tomato sauce (see page 12)

handful of basil, leaves chopped

125g (4oz) mozzarella ball

extra-virgin olive oil

salt and pepper

Here's how

Pre-heat the oven to 180°C/350°F/Gas Mark 4.

Add the gnocchi to a pan of boiling salted water; when they start to rise to the surface of the water they're cooked. Tip them into a colander to drain.

Put the gnocchi back in the saucepan, add the tomato sauce and chopped basil and stir, then spoon into an ovenproof dish.

Squeeze the mozzarella to remove any liquid. Tear it up into chunks and scatter on top of the gnocchi. Drizzle with a little extra-virgin olive oil. Season then pop the dish in the oven for 15 minutes until golden.

Winter minestrone

You can always give a winter vegetable soup a hint of summer simply by stirring in some pesto. Double up the recipe quantities and you'll have enough for tomorrow's lunch at home or to take to work in a flask.

INGREDIENTS

1 medium onion

2 carrots

2 celery sticks

3 garlic cloves

½ a celeriac – about 500g (1lb)

2 tbsp olive oil

sea salt

100ml (3½fl oz) red wine

2 x 400g (13oz) cans of tomatoes

600ml (1 pint) vegetable stock

75g (3oz) spaghetti

2 tbsp homemade basil pesto, to serve (see page 17)

75g (3oz) Parmesan, grated, to serve

Here's how

Peel and dice all the vegetables, including the garlic. Put them in a pan on a medium heat with the olive oil and a sprinkle of sea salt. Cook for about 5 minutes, then add the red wine, followed by the canned tomatoes and stock. Bring the soup to the boil, then turn it down to a gentle simmer.

After 15 minutes, break up the spaghetti into little pieces and throw it into the soup. Give it a stir and leave to finish cooking for another 10 minutes.

When the vegetables and pasta are cooked, serve up the soup with a nice dollop of pesto and a sprinkle of Parmesan.

Celeriac & bacon

Celeriac is a great winter vegetable, but people often ask me what to do with it – usually when they've found one in their weekly vegetable box. My advice is that you can do pretty much anything that you usually do with a potato – and more. Here's one way of using celeriac.

INGREDIENTS

375g (12oz) farfalle pasta

1 celeriac weighing about 1kg (2lb)

2 tbsp extra-virgin olive oil, plus extra to serve

salt and pepper

4 rashers of pancetta or smoked streaky bacon

handful of flat-leaf parsley, chopped

4 cloves of roasted garlic (see page 14)

75g (3oz) Parmesan or Pecorino, shaved, to serve

Here's how

Cook the pasta in a large pan of boiling salted water.

While the pasta is cooking, peel and dice the celeriac. Heat a frying pan and add the celeriac with the olive oil. Season with a little salt and pepper. Dice the bacon and add to the pan. Chop the rosemary and add that too. Cook until the celeriac has softened, stirring occasionally. Squeeze the roasted garlic cloves into the pan while the celeriac is cooking.

Drain the cooked pasta in a colander and shake the last few drips of cooking water into the frying pan to help make a sauce.

Mix in the pasta and serve with a drizzle of extra-virgin olive oil and shavings of Parmesan or Pecorino.

Poor man's Parmesan

When there's no Parmesan in the fridge to finish off your dish, don't worry. Try this recipe instead – it may well change the way you eat pasta! It's amazing what you can do with a few simple store-cupboard ingredients.

INGREDIENTS

375g (12oz) pasta

3 garlic cloves

1 small chilli

3 slices of bread

3 salted anchovy fillets

3 tbsp extra-virgin olive oil, plus extra to finish

salt and pepper

handful of basil

Here's how

Cook the pasta in a large pan of boiling salted water.

While the pasta is cooking, peel the garlic cloves and deseed the chilli. Place the bread, garlic, chilli and anchovies in a food processor and blend to a fine crumb.

Pour the olive oil into a frying pan and cook the breadcrumb mixture on a gentle heat until golden.

Drain the cooked pasta in a colander. As you drain it, whip the pan under the colander to catch the last few drips of the cooking water so that the pasta isn't too dry.

Tip the pasta back into the pan, season with salt, pepper and a little olive oil before sprinkling with the crispy breadcrumbs and tearing the basil leaves on top.

Sautéed Brussels sprouts, cream, garlic & pine nuts

Brussels sprouts – you either love them or hate them. Though I've made some converts with this dish. Once again, I'm convinced this dish works because the sprouts are disguised – they're shredded finely and harder to recognise!

INGREDIENTS

375g (12oz) pasta

250g (8oz) Brussels sprouts

2tbsp olive oil

50g (2oz) butter

1 garlic clove

100ml (3½fl oz) double cream

salt and pepper

squeeze of lemon juice

3 tbsp toasted pine nuts

Here's how

Cook the pasta in a large pan of boiling salted water.

While the pasta is cooking, shred the sprouts as finely as you can. Place a non-stick pan on the heat and add the olive oil and butter. Add the sprouts. Peel and crush the garlic and add that too. Cook for 3–4 minutes until the sprouts start to soften. Add the cream and cook for a further 3–4 minutes on a low heat.

Season with salt, pepper and a squeeze of lemon juice.

Drain the cooked pasta and add to the sprouts, followed by the toasted pine nuts.

Artichokes & black olives

Raiding your local deli is the key to this recipe: a few clever purchases can bring a pasta dish to life. So stop off on your way home or nip out in your lunch hour to pick up the ingredients for this super-fast and super-delicious supper.

INGREDIENTS

375g (12oz) pasta

4 ladlefuls – about 350ml (12fl oz) – of basic tomato sauce (see page 12)

150g (5oz) tub pitted black olives

150g (5oz) tub grilled artichokes

handful of basil

extra-virgin olive oil, to serve

salt and pepper

Here's how

Cook the pasta in a large pan of boiling salted water. Tip the cooked pasta into a colander and stand it in the sink to drain.

Add the tomato sauce to the pasta pan. Warm the sauce through on a low heat. Add the olives and artichokes, followed by the cooked pasta.

Serve in a big bowl with lots of freshly torn basil, good olive oil and a few twists of black pepper.

Hot smoked salmon

I love smoked salmon. Its wonderful smoky flavour can permeate through a dish so easily. This recipe can be made in a flash and yet it tastes – and looks – so classy. This will definitely impress guests on a weekday evening.

INGREDIENTS

375g (12oz) pasta

150ml (¼ pint) crème fraîche

6 sorrel leaves, chopped

squeeze of lemon juice

2 hot smoked salmon fillets, about 225g (7½oz) each

salt and pepper

150g (5oz) baby spinach, to serve

Here's how

Cook the pasta in a large pan of boiling salted water. Tip the cooked pasta into a colander and stand it in the sink to drain.

Add the crème fraîche, chopped sorrel leaves and a squeeze of lemon juice to the pasta pan. Break the hot smoked salmon into the sauce, then add the cooked pasta. Give it a good stir around, have a taste and season with salt and pepper.

Put the baby spinach in a bowl and serve the pasta on top.

Arrabiata sauce

This is a lovely rich tomato sauce with a devilish kick of chilli – sounds good to me! Keep a jar of pickled chillies in your fridge and you won't have to mess about deseeding fresh ones – pickling them reduces the heat but none of the flavour.

INGREDIENTS

375g (12oz) pasta

4 ladlefuls – about 350ml (12fl oz) – of basic tomato sauce (see page 12)

3 pickled chillies

handful of basil, leaves chopped

50g (2oz) Parmesan, grated

extra-virgin olive oil

Here's how

Cook the pasta in a large pan of boiling salted water. Tip the cooked pasta into a colander and stand it in the sink to drain.

Add the tomato sauce to the pasta pan. Chop the pickled chillies finely and add to the sauce. Heat the sauce gently for a few minutes, then stir in the cooked pasta and the chopped basil.

Serve with grated Parmesan and a drizzle of extra-virgin olive oil.

Index

Acknowledgements

I would like to thank my fantastic wife Emma and beautiful daughter Poppy for their love and support. Without them I would not be able to achieve half of what I set out to do.

Thanks to my parents and my mother- and father-in-law. I am very lucky to have two sets of parents to help and support me.

A special thank-you goes to Dan Grimshaw, my assistant/chef/business partner and good friend, who is always there in the thick of it, helping me.

Peter Sidwell

Conversion tables

Weights

15g	½oz
25g	1oz
50g	2oz
75g	3oz
100g	3½oz
125g	4oz
150g	5oz
175g	6oz
200g	7oz
225g	7½oz
250g	8oz
275g	9oz
300g	10oz
375g	12oz
400g	13oz
450g	14oz
475g	15oz
500g	1lb
625g	1¼lb
750g	1½lb
1kg	2lb
1.25kg	2½lb
1.5kg	3lb
1.75kg	3½lb
2kg	4lb

Liquid Measurements

5ml	1 tsp
15ml	1 tbsp or ½ fl oz
25ml	1fl oz
50ml	2fl oz or ¼ cup
75ml	3fl oz
100ml	3½fl oz
125ml	4fl oz or ½ cup
150ml	5fl oz (¼ pint)
175ml	6fl oz
200ml	7fl oz
225ml	7½fl oz
250ml	8fl oz or 1 cup
275ml	9fl oz
300ml	½ pint or 1¼ cups
450ml	¾ pint
600ml	1 pt (20 fl oz)
1 litre	1¾ pints

Oven temperatures

°C	°F	Gas Mark	Oven
110	225	¼	
120	250	½	
140	275	1	Cool
150	300	2	
160	325	3	Moderate
180	350	4	
190	375	5	Moderately Hot
200	400	6	
220	425	7	Hot
230	450	8	
240	475	9	Very Hot

NB Cooking times for fan assisted ovens may be shorter. Please refer to manufacturers guidelines. All conversions are approximate.